Praise for RABBIS TALK ABOUT INTERMARRIAGE

Rabbis are on the forefront of the of the intermarriage issue.
They are asked to officiate at the wedding ceremonies, meet with
the couple and console distraught parents. They feel the impact
of intermarriage in their synagogues and their families, even in
the authority of their vocation.

Gary Tobin and Kathy Simon have wisely listened to the rabbis
discuss their conflicts and their struggles and they have present-
ed an important window to understanding one of the most
important issues of the Jewish future. They have been fair and
honest; the eloquence of the book belongs to the rabbis whose
views are represented so sensitively and so keenly. One sees how
much rabbis of each denomination share in common and how
deep their struggle to grapple with the changing demographics
of the American Jewish community.

One can easily imagine that a century from now, this will be a
central work documenting the transformation of American
Jewry as it enters the new Millennia. *Rabbis Talk About
Intermarriage* is a seminal work worthy of much discussion, one
that asks so many important questions and seeks authentic
answers.

— MICHAEL BERENBAUM
Professor of Theology (Adjunct)
The University of Judaism

RABBIS TALK
ABOUT
INTERMARRIAGE

RABBIS TALK
ABOUT
INTERMARRIAGE

GARY A. TOBIN
KATHERINE G. SIMON

INSTITUTE FOR
JEWISH & COMMUNITY
RESEARCH
SAN FRANCISCO

Library of Congress Catalog Card Number: 9 9 - 7 6 5 6 0

I S B N :   1 - 8 9 3 6 7 1 - 0 0 - 3

This book is printed on recycled acid-free paper that contains at least 20 percent postconsumer waste.

PRINTED IN THE UNITED STATES OF AMERICA

03 02 01 00 99   5 4 3 2 1

CONTENTS

DEDICATION

This book is dedicated

to the memory of

Bruce Kaufman

PREFACE

A RAPIDLY CHANGING WORLD

Nearly all Jews have an opinion and all Jews have a stake concerning intermarriage. Even Jews who opt out of the Jewish community make a choice that not only affects their own lives but the community as a whole. Each member of the tribe is considered precious and irreplaceable. Most Jews understand that they individually represent a small part of a tiny religious minority, both in the United States and the world as a whole. Already diminished by the extermination wrought by the Holocaust, Jews wonder about their survival as a legitimate and viable community. Passions about intermarriage, debates about how to prevent it or reap benefits from its consequences have at their core a genuine concern about group survival.

People who marry out of Judaism can be pessimistically viewed as defectors, lost opportunities or individual actors in Judaism's self-destruction. Or, optimistically, they may be viewed as the renewers of the faith — those who will bolster Jewish numbers and strength by bringing in "new blood" and building the Jewish community through addition rather than constriction. In either case, the phenomenon of intermarriage embodies both a personal and philosophical concern with the identity of Jews, the preservation of a distinct peoplehood, and the history and future of Judaism. Rabbis are by definition at the center of these issues.

The debates about intermarriage in the 1990s come at a time when the nature of the Jewish community worldwide has changed dramatically, allowing the American Jewish community to engage in its most serious contemplation about its identity, structure and overall future. For decades, the Jewish community had been in a crisis mode about building Israel and rescuing Soviet Jewry. Tremendous energy was turned to concerns about security in Israel, the building of the State, the threat to Israel's existence from its hostile neighbors and the financial needs of Israel. At the same time, a great fervor was generated over the release and then the mass migration of Jews from the former Soviet Union. The exodus of more than three-quarters of a million Jews from Russia, Ukraine and the other former Soviet Republics was the result of a massive political and financial campaign on behalf of the Jewish community. The ability of Jews to migrate from the former Soviet Union to Israel, based on self-selection and economic concerns rather than on restrictions placed by the former Soviet government, reduced the sense of crisis among American Jews to financially support the migration and resettlement of Jews from the former Soviet Republics in both Israel and the United States. At the same time, the development of peace in the Middle East and the growing prosperity of Israel created a sense of security for Israel. The two great crises that had dominated American Jewish consciousness — the concern about Israel's safety and survival and the repression and captivity of Jews in the former Soviet Union — became far less dominant in the mid-1990s. For the first time since the Holocaust, American Jews felt free to contemplate their own community, the meaning of Jewish life in America and the gravity of internal threats to the American Jewish community (as opposed to external threats to other Jewish communities around the world).

In a great historical juxtaposition, the 1990s also saw the Jewish community inundated by information about intermarriage. The 1990 National Jewish Population Survey spawned a deluge of analysis and commentary about intermarriage in both the scholarly journals and the popular Jewish press. Next to news concerning Israel, and specifically the peace process, discussions about and analyses of intermarriage became more dominant than any other subject in the American Jewish press. Local Jewish newspapers regularly run stories about incidences of anti-semitism, and major newspapers such as the *New York Times* or *Los Angeles Times* regularly report on Passover and *Chanukah.* But discussions about the future of the Jewish people, group survival, Jewish education and the whole range of issues that are ultimately linked to discussions of intermarriage began to dominate editorials and general news reporting within the Jewish community. In the wake of the 1990 study, practically every Jewish community formed a Jewish continuity commission, or task force, or some other communal entity that dealt with the survival of the Jewish people based on internal threats of unstoppable assimilation and the possibility that Jews would intermarry themselves into oblivion.

The data for this analysis come from a variety of sources. First, personal interviews were conducted with over 30 rabbis in Northern California between 1992 and 1994, and follow-up questions were asked in 1995 and 1996. Most of the rabbis interviewed were congregational rabbis, although a small number also served in bureaus of Jewish education, community relations councils or other Jewish organizations. A small number of the rabbis had no denominational or organizational affiliation, and were essentially "community" rabbis who officiated at baby namings, funerals, weddings and High Holiday services. The personal interviews averaged approximately two hours, and covered a wide range of issues including attitudes and beliefs about assimilation, philosophies of Jewish education and feelings about intermarriage. Many rabbis did not want to be quoted. Therefore, many of the references refer only to Orthodox, Conservative or Reform as identification.

A second source of qualitative data was a content analysis of sermons delivered by rabbis at their congregations or in other settings. About 70 sermons were analyzed. The sermons came from a wide variety of rabbis in congregations and other organizations throughout the United States, and broadly represented Orthodox, Conservative, Reform and Reconstructionist views. The sermons offer a slightly different rabbinic perspective since these writings were designed for public consumption and review. Sermons are delivered to educate, guide, lead or inspire. They state norms, visions and prohibitions. The sermons differ both in tone and style from the introspective views from the one-on-one personal interviews to the intensity of the conference proceedings.

A third source of qualitative data comes from articles, monographs or essays written by rabbis. Articles written about intermarriage and related subjects were collected. The most interesting discussions of intermarriage took place after the release of the 1990 National Jewish Population Survey, and its revelation of a stated intermarriage rate of over 50 percent.

Data are also drawn from two surveys administered to Northern California rabbis in 1992 and 1995. The surveys covered a broad range of issues concerning the role of the rabbi and the synagogue, the Jewish community, policies to address assimilation and the changing character of Jewish life. The sermons and essays of rabbis from all over the United States revealed no difference from the views found in Northern California.

It is important to note that the qualitative data — personal interviews and content analysis of sermons — do not represent a statistically representative survey of the views of American rabbis.

This book does not purport to say that "x" percent of Orthodox rabbis or "y" percent of Reform rabbis have certain beliefs or behaviors concerning intermarriage. Rather, qualitative sources are utilized to provide an in-depth look at what rabbis say and how they feel about the issue of intermarriage, utilizing their own words. Qualitative data also allow us to look at the subtleties and nuances about rabbinic beliefs and feelings concerning intermarriage in ways that quantitative research may oversimplify. The issue of intermarriage is so complicated and emotional for most rabbis that the categorical responses found in quantitative research would not necessarily help unravel their complex and often contradictory feelings and beliefs.

The focus on intermarriage as a primal concern with group survival derives from the use of intermarriage as the primary measure that Jews utilize to judge the future of the group.

People may bemoan the lack of participation in synagogues or declining levels of ritual observance, or ignorance about Jewish history or religious tradition, but with far less passion than intermarriage. After all, if Jews are still marrying other Jews (even if they do not behave much like Jews), most Jews seem to be content that ultimate group survival is not in question.

Reactions to intermarriage tend to be negative and crisis-oriented. A series of articles in *Moment* magazine, in which Jewish sociologists, demographers and planners debated fiercely with each other about the National Jewish Population Survey, reveals the high communal stakes that are associated with discussions of intermarriage. One sociologist, Steven M. Cohen of The Hebrew University, claims that the intermarriage rate is 42%, not 52%, while most of those associated with the National Jewish Population Survey defend their findings that the rate of intermarriage is 52%. Cohen argues that there is a tremendous psychological barrier that is broken by putting forward an intermarriage rate of 52%, while others argue that 42% is already high and growing, and should be of enough concern that the percentage differences are irrelevant.[1] The fierceness of the interchange among the scholars has much to do with the fact that they are discussing intermarriage and not rates of Jewish education or patterns of residential migration. They believe that they are discussing the future of group survival of the Jewish community in America.[2] Rabbis are at the center of these discussions.

---

[1] Steven M. Cohen, "Why Intermarriage May Not Threaten Jewish Continuity," Moment, December 1994, 54-57.

[2] Sidney Goldstein, et al., "Twelve Angry Men and Women," Moment, April 1995, 66-69.

ACKNOWLEDGMENTS

I would like to thank my co-author, Kathy Simon. She was a creative collaborator and a challenging thinker throughout the process. The Max and Anna Levinson Foundation provided seed money for the project and the Koret Foundation also supported this endeavor. All of the rabbis who participated in this study — those who were interviewed, filled out surveys and sent in their sermons and other writings — deserve our gratitude. Their cooperation is another indication of their love, concern and effort on behalf of the Jewish people.

Most of all, I would like to thank Arlene Kaufman. Her dedication to the work of the Institute for Jewish & Community Research made this project possible. This book could not have been completed without her generous support.

Gary A. Tobin

RABBIS TALK
ABOUT
INTERMARRIAGE

CHAPTER ONE

RABBIS AND THE INTERMARRIAGE DEBATE

THE RABBI IN THE EYE OF THE STORM

Intermarriage is a powerful, active force in the consciousness of most rabbis: They are compelled to think about intermarriage more than any other group of individuals in Jewish life. Yet their own personal and family experiences make them think and feel about intermarriage in much the same ways as other Jews. The nature of the rabbis' profession requires them to deal with intermarriage on a daily basis: weddings, birth, burial and other major and small decisions concerning Jews and non-Jews. Others may choose to ignore the issue or deny its importance, or simply accept it with indifference, hope or disappointment. Congregational rabbis face daily decisions about whether or not to perform wedding ceremonies with intermarried couples, how to counsel interfaith couples, what they will teach their congregants about intermarriage, how interfaith families fit into the synagogue, and so on. Actions about intermarriage are a part of everyday life in one way or another.

Rabbis are the keepers of the faith in contemporary Jewish life. They are expected to provide the knowledge, guidelines and moral strength to help transmit Judaism from one generation to the next. While most observers acknowledge that the family should be the desired primary transmitter of Jewish values and identity, almost all students of Jewish life acknowledge that the rabbi is a key communal influence to enliven and preserve that Jewish identity. Many Jewish families have little to offer the next generation in the way of Jewish knowledge, meaning or inspiration. Jewish organizations and institutions — particularly the synagogue — must play the role of family. Group survival is dependent on cohesion — at least to some degree — through common history and ideology. Rabbis can provide some linkages through information and guidance.

What rabbis do and think matters. The standards they set, positions they advocate, actions they take, all have a cumulative, profound impact on the structure and character of Jewish life. Because the Jewish community is now more disjointed and more disconnected than in previous eras, the role of the rabbis looms even larger. The fate of Jewish survival is too heavy a burden to place in their hands. But the direction and character of Judaism can be profoundly influenced by how they think and how they behave. All of the actors in this complex institutional and social network have an intuitive understanding that the role of the rabbi can be significant and influential in redefining Judaism. Therefore, how rabbis deal with intermarriage affects the quality of individual Jewish lives and Judaism in general.

Many rabbis participate at the center of the intermarriage debate with a great deal of enthusiasm. Rabbis are playing an increasingly prominent role in communal influence outside the synagogue. Their moral authority is now more legitimate in the face of an intermarriage "crisis." When the Jewish press filled with news about an intermarriage rate of 52%, the rabbinate stepped forward to say a great deal about the subject.

Their views are naturally divergent. There are multiple ideas about why intermarriage occurs, how it should be prevented, how it should be embraced, how it represents the ruin of the Jewish people or the hope for the Jewish people, how Jewish education will solve the "intermarriage problem," how outreach will build upon the positive aspects of integration into American society and make intermarriage a fruitful experience of positive growth rather than one of dismay. Rabbis can be found all along the spectrum of possible ideologies and approaches, seeing intermarriage as either a tremendous threat, a problem to be managed or a wonderful opportunity for American Jews. But intermarriage is rarely discussed as an isolated phenomenon of Jews marrying non-Jews, or as a sociological phenomenon of the *present*. The discussion is almost always framed by the future, the upbringing of children and grandchildren, and therefore the future generations of Jews that may or may not exist.

How Rabbis Think about Intermarriage

Rabbis think and feel about intermarriage through a number of lenses. The first lens is individual and personal. Their experiences, both positive and negative, strongly influence their views of intermarriage. Did their parents forbid them to date non-Jews? Did they fall in love with someone who was not Jewish and choose not to marry him or her? Or conversely, did they themselves marry someone who converted to Judaism, or in rare cases, marry someone who was not Jewish?

Formative experiences in their own familial relationships color subsequent feelings and behaviors. Rabbis deal with intermarriage on a personal level. They are concerned about their own children, grandchildren and other members of their family. How do they react to their own children dating non-Jews or marrying non-Jews? What if a child's spouse converts or does not convert? The pervasiveness of intermarriage affects rabbis' families as it affects all Jews. Rabbis think about intermarriage not only because they are rabbis, but also as parents and grandparents, uncles and aunts, brothers and sisters. Being a rabbi does not make them immune from the conflicts, confusion and wide range of other emotions that most Jews experience in dealing with intermarriage. Like many American Jews, they are faced with personal choices and dilemmas about intermarriage. All of these experiences, either consciously or unconsciously, influence the ways that any particular rabbi views intermarriage.

The second view is communal. Rabbis view intermarriage as communal leaders who are concerned about the future of the Jewish community. These attitudes are the most public. Rabbis believe that the community has a particularly high stake in the rabbinic role, that they are "the keepers of the faith." The future of the community can be greatly influenced by what they say and how they behave. When rabbis voice their feelings as community leaders, they see themselves as representatives of the Jewish people with a sense of responsibility to future generations of Jews. Such a perspective, of course, carries with it a remarkable sense of responsibility, which can be both empowering and burdensome.

Some rabbis are able to articulate the difference between their personal views and their communal views. They may believe on a personal basis, for example, that intermarriage is either acceptable or at least not catastrophic, while their communal view can claim just the opposite. There can be dissonance between the "I" when the rabbis speak for themselves, and the "we" when they put forward a position on behalf of the Jewish community.

The third view is ideological or theological. Rabbis state views as commands or restrictions that they see defined by prescriptive or interpretive law. They interpret God's will or intention. Arguments made in this realm are impossible to debate except within the internal structure of these religious paradigms. Some rabbis believe they are acting to keep Jews a unique people of the covenant and, further, they believe that this covenant is defined through birth rather than by choice (with rare and difficult exceptions).

Approaches to intermarriage for these rabbis can produce both strong and rigid opposition to intermarriage. Some rabbis may retreat behind interpretations of the law as a means to avoid either their own communal or personal views of intermarriage. Few of the sermons or the writings of rabbis, however, ever really discuss intermarriage in the context of law. Procedures for conversion are rarely the focus, and the ways conversion provides for the acceptance of non-Jews into Judaism are almost never discussed. Mechanisms for making non-Jews part of the Jewish faith do exist. Therefore, theological objections to intermarriage are actually rabbis' views of how intermarriage affects the character and substance of the Jewish community.

The fourth view is denominational. Each movement has a set of guidelines, philosophies and procedures either explicit or normative in terms of intermarriage. The denominations themselves are key players in this intermarriage saga of Jews in the United States. Conservative and Orthodox Jews, for example, argue that they have been correct in warning of the impending internal "holocaust" from the onslaught of intermarriage. The only hope for the future of American Jewry, they tend to argue, is a return to authentic Judaism as defined by Orthodoxy or as close to Orthodoxy as right-wing Conservative Judaism can be. The Reform movement, of course, along with the Reconstructionists (as an alternative religious movement within Judaism) assert that outreach and inclusiveness are the best mechanisms to deal with intermarriage, and therefore the legitimate hope for the survival of the Jewish people in America rests more in their liberal ideology than in the more rigid approaches of prevention or rejection.

Working within a denominational system, rabbis may either promote or retreat behind the denominational philosophy as a means of reinforcing their personal or communal feelings. For example, denominational ideology or guidelines may offer some institutional protection for some rabbis within their congregations. Rabbis who do not wish to perform intermarriage wedding ceremonies can ascribe their decision to denominational constraints. Conversely, these rules may also tie a rabbi's hands, particularly Conservative or Orthodox rabbis who may have more liberal personal ideologies. Denominational constraints may help insulate a rabbi from his/her own conflicted feelings about how to deal with a particular issue. The denominational view, therefore, may be both a blessing and a curse, liberating rabbis from individual choice and confusion or binding them to personally undesirable behaviors.

The fifth view is congregational. Synagogues claim the most authoritative and central role in the hierarchy of Jewish organizations and institutions as the bulwark against intermarriage and as the institutional hope for continuity in Jewish life. The rabbi may be pulled or pushed in a particular direction on a given intermarriage issue, responding to various political pressures within the congregation. For many, the congregational view centers upon whether or not rabbis will perform wedding ceremonies between Jews and non-Jews. The debates about wedding ceremonies take place between rabbis within denominations, between denominations and between rabbis and families of those who approach them. The debate, of course, is most salient in Reform congregations where there is individual rabbinic discretion about performing intermarriage ceremonies. There is less pressure from congregants within the Conservative congregations for rabbis to perform intermarriages. The debate is almost closed for Orthodox rabbis, where there is little individual or ideological debate about the approach of the rabbinate to intermarriage.

Congregational views may reflect denominational guidelines, but these may be open to multiple shades of interpretation, especially within the Reform movement. Alternately, since not all rabbis have well-defined denominational allegiances, in spite of their ordination, the congregational view may be largely defined by the interaction of the rabbi and the congregants. Congregational ideologies may be formulated with the rabbi's guidance or may have been formulated before the rabbi joined that particular congregation. Therefore the rabbi is in a position of either endorsing or ceding to a particular congregational set of ideologies and practices, or trying to move them in another direction. Either way, the view of the rabbi may be influenced or constrained by the congregational view.

Some rabbis point out that the norms about intermarriage have changed. Intermarriage was seen as an aberration in previous generations of Jews, either a form of rebellion against parents and community, or the behavior of someone who had lost his or her way. Today, however, intermarriage is seen as part of the fabric of everyday life of American Jews, stemming partly from their general integration into American society. In some cases, intermarriage may still occur as a form of rebellion as children attempt to differentiate themselves from parents or extended families. But for the most part, the phenomenon is linked more to its general acceptability that arises from the minimal levels of Jewish life in which most American Jewish families are now engaged. In other words, many rabbis believe that children are given so little grounding in Jewish life through ritual observance, synagogue attendance and other familial and community bonds, that these children reflect their parents' disinterest in Judaism.

It is clear to many rabbis that the nature of contemporary American life fosters intermarriage, even among those with strong Jewish identities. Children are raised in the American liberal ideology. Everyone is equal and emphasis on racial, religious or cultural differences can be viewed as bigoted. Jews raised in a liberal tradition believe that religious or ethnic differentiation may be the same as unnecessary tribalism. Some rabbis actually promote intermarriage as a means of breaking down barriers of all kinds. Marriage between Jews and non-Jews, therefore, is seen by some as a logical outcome of cultural liberalism and in some sense is desirable as a means to overcome prejudice. This assimilationist view, largely held prior to the 1950s, is rarely voiced among contemporary rabbis.

A number of rabbis believe that the institutional approach to dealing with intermarriage is much the same as dealing with the Jewish population as a whole. Some indicate that the levels of knowledge about Judaism and participation in Jewish life among born Jews is so low that the process of teaching and outreach are almost identical between Jews and non-Jews. Some rabbis contend that many Jews who are in-married are as disconnected from Jewish life as those who are intermarried, and that the quality of Jewish life as a whole is in jeopardy, regardless of whether or not intermarriage rates decrease, remain the same or rise.

The prevention versus outreach ideologies have nuances and subtexts. For example, some rabbis call for proselytizing among disaffected non-Jews, the "unchurched" or spiritually seeking, particularly in the Christian world. Given that intermarriage is inevitable, they argue, and the community must replace its losses, some contend that the recruitment of new members is as important as the retention of old members. The ideology of proselytizing is based in the notion that Judaism is a religious identity that can be achieved by multiple routes including birth or conversion. At the heart of the proselytizing ideology is the tenet that the size of the Jewish population is important. While each individual Jewish life or soul is considered valuable, the vibrancy and quality of Jewish life is also seen as partially determined by the numbers of people who call themselves Jews. Proselytizing calls for the conversion of non-Jews in the general society who may be interested in becoming Jewish. The totality of the group identity, therefore, is determined less by lineage and more by the conscious choice to become a Jew. In this ideology, intermarriage becomes an opportunity, not a problem. Switching moves in either direction — non-Jewish to Jewish as well as the other way around. Some Jews may choose to marry non-Jews and remove themselves from Jewish life. Others may marry a non-Jewish partner and choose a Jewish identity. Taken to a logical next step, the size of the Jewish population could actually grow by the active promotion of Judaism. If some choose to marry out and abandon their identity, their losses will be more than compensated for by the addition of new Jews who have actively chosen a Jewish religious identity.

The ideology of proselytizing is endorsed by few rabbis. Outreach and integration, the calls for the active promotion of Judaism to individuals who have entered the realm of the Jewish community through marriage to a Jewish partner, are advocated by many rabbis. It includes the active promotion of Judaism to the children of intermarried couples. The ideology is bound less in prevention and more in recovery. This is not to say that those who embrace the ideology of outreach and integration abandon the ideology of prevention, but rather see it as a part of a multiple strategy that attempts to build a strong Jewish identity as a bulwark against intermarriage on the one hand and minimizing potential loss by outreach and integration on the other hand. Those who advocate the ideology of outreach and integration believe they have some influence on the ultimate Jewish identity of the children of intermarried households, either through the active recruitment of the non-Jewish spouse or the children themselves. The adoption of this ideology may lead to a particular set of behaviors such as performing wedding ceremonies for intermarried couples, active counseling or education in Judaism for non-Jewish spouses. The extent to which individual rabbis attempt to reach out and the methods that they use are not clearly defined.

Most rabbis embrace the ideology of prevention. Even those who are more open to various methods of outreach and integration believe that a strong Jewish education, a strong statement of family norms, either in favor of inmarriage or prohibiting intermarriage, and active involvement of the family in Jewish life are all deterrents to intermarriage. The prevention ideology calls for a whole range of structural and programmatic and institutional actions that will either encourage inmarriage or serve as barriers to intermarriage. The ideology of prevention rests primarily in advocacy for Jewish education, both formal and informal. Other programmatic avenues are also seen as positive, including mechanisms for Jews to meet other Jews, especially in marrying years, or efforts to strengthen the fabric of Jewish community life as a whole. Most of the emphasis, however, is on education and a belief that identity as a Jew and resistance to intermarriage are strongly correlated.

The Evolving Role of the Rabbi

Many rabbis believe that they must educate and set the norms for the community. Rabbis often expect themselves to be voices of conscience in the Jewish community to help guide and mold identities and behaviors. This is not a false or immodest self-perception. Rabbis interact with individuals and families in an authoritative way in most life-cycle events such as birth, marriage and death.

Congregations and seminaries play roles as institutions but these, of course, are largely influenced by the rabbis themselves. Individual philanthropists play some role, either through federations, foundations or other institutions by funding outreach or other programs. Academics, particularly Jewish studies scholars, sociologists, anthropologists and historians can also influence the way people think about intermarriage. But scholars do not tend to interact with individuals on an everyday basis. While the overall ideologies and understanding of intermarriage may be affected by the scholarly world, the one-on-one interaction of rabbis with congregants and other members of the Jewish community has a much more substantial impact on the lives of individual Jews. Families themselves — grandparents, parents and children — are the most important decision-makers of all since intermarriage results from the totality of individual decisions. Each micro decision is made in a macro system. Rabbinic attitudes can have a major cumulative effect.

Congregations may have policies about what role, if any, non-Jewish spouses or children of intermarried couples can play in worship services. Congregations may also determine the extent to which, if any, they may hold leadership positions as voting members of the synagogue, having children of intermarried couples become *bar* or *bat mitzvah* (celebration signifying entry into the covenant) or confirmed, and other such structural, procedural and philosophical issues. The congregation may turn to the rabbi, or conversely, the rabbi may be assertive in a leadership position to help guide or adjudicate in many of these decisions. How the rabbi feels may influence the direction of the synagogue on particular rules, both formal and informal.

The marriage ceremony (and rabbis' involvement or non-involvement) is only one of many potential intervention points for the rabbi in dealing with intermarriage. Personal and ideological views enter the lives of Jews in many ways. For example, what does the religious school teach about intermarriage? Is the subject approached at all, either formally or informally, through specific curricula or special discussions at weekend retreats? Is there an overall philosophy about the congregational approach to intermarriage that is incorporated into the educational process, and does the rabbi play a role in determining that philosophy?

**Comparison of Central Conference of American Rabbis
(CCAR) and Reconstructionist Rabbinical Association (RRA)
Respondents (1995)**

Position	CCAR		RRA		CCAR RRA Total	
	#	%	#	%	#	%
Officiate	318	48%	24	38%	334	47%
Refer	245	37%	32	51%	274	39%
Do not refer	96	15%	7	11%	102	14%
Total Respondents	659	100%	63	100%	710*	100%

Whether or not rabbis will perform intermarriage cere-monies is only one of many issues (albeit the most prominent issue for congregants and non-congregants alike) that rabbis deal with every day concerning intermarriage. The officiation issue remains a key intermarriage battleground for rabbis and is dis-cussed often in the literature.[3] Some research has actually been done concerning rates of rabbinic officiation at intermarriage ceremonies. A study by Rabbi Irwin Fishbein in 1995 s h o w e d that 48% of Reform rabbis and 38% of Reconstructionist rabbis

---

[3] See Henry Cohen, "Promises, Promises." *Moment,* February 1997, pp. 56-57, and Harry K. Danziger, "Why I Officiate at Selected Interfaith Weddings." *Reform Judaism,* Fall, 1996, pp. 52-54.
*The total number of respondents, as well as the total number for each posi-tion, differs from the sum of CCAR (Central Conference of American Rabbis) and RRA (Reconstructionist Rabbinical Association) respondents because the affiliation of three respondents is not known and fourteen respondents belong to both organizations.

officiate at interfaith weddings. About 14% neither officiate nor refer a couple to another rabbi who will officiate (see Table 1).[4]

The role of the rabbi is best summarized by Rabbi Fishbein when he dismisses the officiation issue as overblown and discusses instead the guiding, teaching, and counseling role that a rabbi can serve:

> Whether a rabbi officiates or does not officiate or what conditions he puts upon his officiating, may be less critical for the couple than whether the rabbi can respond to them openly, distinguish between his values and theirs and help them evaluate the decision they are about to make in terms of individual family and community.[5]

Even if the marriage ceremony dilemma were completely resolved, a whole range of other intermarriage issues would remain. The intermarriage ceremony allows everyone to have a convenient focal point for fears, anger, regret, blame, hope and confusion concerning the marriage of Jews and non-Jews. The stakes are high, but not substantially different than circumcisions, baby namings, entrance to religious school, congregational membership or burials. While everyone would seem relieved if the marriage ceremony issue were resolved, the emotional focus would likely shift to some other arena. The role of the rabbi would continue to be critical and criticized, supported or condemned with the same passion. The real issues are centered in the adjustment of the realities of intermarriage in an assimilated Jewish culture. Yet, whether or not rabbis should or should not perform intermarriage ceremonies is not the focus of this vol-

---

[4] Irwin H. Fishbein, *Rabbinic Participation in Intermarriage Ceremonies.* Summary of Rabbinic Center for Research and Counseling 1995 Survey, 29 December 1995.

[5] Irwin Fishbein, *Intermarriage and Outreach: Facing Contemporary Challenges.* 24th Annual Convention of the Federation of Reconstructionist Congregations and Havurot, 14 June 1984.

ume. While it is a subject of concern and is discussed in the analysis, this is not a book about the performing of intermarriage wedding ceremonies. Although mixed-marriage wedding ceremonies are not the central focus of this analysis, the subject comes up very often as the rabbis themselves talk about intermarriage. Like their lay counterparts, rabbis also focus on the wedding ceremony when thinking about and discussing intermarriage.

THE GROWING ROLE OF THE RABBI

The decentralization of Jewish communal life continues, mirroring changes in contemporary American society with the proliferation of religious choices and types, the growth of small groups and the mushrooming of alternative religious ideologies and institutions. Rabbis are increasingly part of growing *havurot* or alternative congregations, where different rules and constructs are created to deal with this growing diversity. These forums may be less secure and professionally unsuitable for some rabbis, but are areas of future institutional growth. The personal feelings and beliefs of rabbis concerning the complex issues surrounding intermarriage may have greater salience and importance in the future. Even within existing institutions, the largest of the denominational movements —Reform — has the most flexibility concerning intermarriage.

Rabbis operate from a multitude of institutions within the Jewish community. Most rabbis operate at the congregational level, deriving their communal influence from their synagogue base. Rabbis also operate in the Jewish community system from a wide variety of venues. They serve as staff of Hillel Foundations on college campuses, coming into contact with tens of thousands of Jewish students. They also serve as the faculty of the seminaries, training future generations of rabbis, or in the national and regional denominational structure. Rabbis also can be found on the faculties of major universities in the growing number of Jewish studies programs that have been created over the past two decades, or in individually endowed chairs. Rabbis also serve in a variety of positions in Jewish communal organizations such as chaplains for hospitals, directors of bureaus of Jewish education and community relations committees, executive directors, planning directors or other positions within federations, and so on. Indeed, a rabbi has recently held the position of chief executive of the United Jewish Appeal, the largest Jewish fundraising organization in the world. Rabbis increasingly find themselves in influential roles as executive directors or advisors of Jewish family foundations and other positions of growing influence in the Jewish community. The rabbinic voice in the Jewish communal system extends far beyond and much deeper than the congregational level. How rabbis think and feel about intermarriage is systemically integral throughout the Jewish institutional and organizational structure.

The rabbi is a powerful influence in the community, yet often feels powerless, as seen in Chapter 2, in dealing with intermarriage. Looking at the overall forces of assimilation or individual decisions that seem beyond their reach or influence, rabbis often feel as if they are fighting a terrible losing battle. These feelings can be reinforced by the community, which often makes the rabbi the focus or receptacle for all of their feelings of confusion, disappointment or anger. But we assume that individuals and groups of individuals influence change. The collective behaviors of rabbis are critically important, even if some rabbis feel powerless.

This discussion is about how rabbis think, feel and behave concerning intermarriage. The analysis revolves around three basic premises. First, rabbis are critical actors in the intermarriage drama which has emerged as the most important issue in contemporary Jewish life. Second, rabbis have a multitude of feelings that affect their behaviors. These feelings are often powerful and contradictory. Third, these feelings translate into behaviors that have profound effects on individual Jews and, collectively, on the Jewish community as a whole.

CHAPTER TWO

RABBIS' FEELINGS ABOUT INTERMARRIAGE

This chapter provides text of the rabbis speaking in their own words about intermarriage. The focus here will be not so much on what the rabbis do with regard to intermarriage and the intermarried couples they work with, but on how they feel. As we shall see, rabbis' feelings range from anguish to delight, from defensiveness to pride, from confusion to self-righteousness. Quotes from personal interviews identify the rabbis' denominations, but not their names.

ANGUISH AND ALARM

Anguish Regarding Intermarriage in General

Probably the most appropriate place to initiate a discussion of feelings aroused among rabbis by current levels of intermarriage is to start, for better or worse, with the feelings of anguish and alarm. Like many others in the Jewish world, many rabbis — across denominational lines — visibly ache when reflecting on the topic. A Conservative rabbi puts it this way:

> I believe it [intermarriage] is the number one threat to Jewish continuity and community far more than the Middle East conflict, and far more than antisemitism (which sometimes draws people closer together). Intermarriage is so quiet and

insidious and nibbles away at the community continuously...I feel bad.

In a similar vein, an Orthodox rabbi expresses his pain at the apparently inevitable losses to the Jewish people caused by intermarriage:

> I see it [intermarriage] as a terrible tragedy. We are losing scores every week to intermarriage around the country. I am seen as very hard line when it comes to intermarriage, but I don't see it as hard lined — I see it as realistic line. It is tragic.

The anguish and hopelessness surrounding intermarriage can go so far that some rabbis believe this is the last generation of Jews in the United States. A Reform rabbi unhappily predicts the complete disintegration of Jewish identity in America:

> We are next to the last Jewish generation in America. That's what I see. Bagels on Sunday morning are not going to save us as a Jewish community. Identifying as Jews will save us and it is dangerous, so why do it. You don't have to convert. You can marry somebody who is not Jewish and go with the flow: "I'll bring my kids up as Christians — Christians are good people, after all, I married one. I sleep with one at night. So what can be so terrible? My kids will be American." It is fatalist, but ... I see the views that Jews in their 40s seem to have of American values — not Jewish values but American values — "Rabbi, you won't see me on Friday night, there is a basketball game." I lose hope.

Another Reform rabbi shares these fears with his colleagues, and sums up their collective sense of foreboding:

> There are times that I feel that Judaism and the Jewish people will barely survive the next 20 years.

While each of the above comments was made privately, the pain, fear and anguish revealed here also finds fervent public expression. When voicing their alarm about intermarriage, rabbis often allude to the Holocaust. The allusion may be used simply to strengthen the admonition that the Jewish people cannot afford to lose any more if its population. Sometimes, though, the rabbis go a step further, suggesting that Hitler would be pleased if he could see what was happening to the Jews in America. In either case, one recognizes the alarm and grief with which the rabbis speak. Rabbi Warmflash (C), speaking to his congregation on *Erev Yom Kippur* (1988), warns plaintively:

...We are a tiny people, only a minute fraction of the world's population. We lost six million in the Holocaust, one-third of our entire people, and we continue to have one of the world's lowest birth rates. We are literally an endangered species. ...

Rabbi Jonathan Ginsburg (C, *Rosh Hashanah* 1991) calls the intermarriage statistics "heartbreaking," and affirms the words of Emil Fackenheim, who "after the Holocaust said that we have to add a 614th commandment, and that would be 'not to grant Hitler a posthumous victory by assimilating.'"

Anguish Regarding the Officiation Decision

The decision about whether or not to officiate at the marriage ceremonies of intermarried couples gives rise to considerable angst among rabbis confronted with that choice. Unlike their Orthodox and Conservative colleagues, who are forbidden by their movements from officiating at mixed-marriages, Reform, Reconstructionist and Jewish Renewal rabbis decide individually about whether or not to officiate. For many of them, that decision bears all the anxiety, uncertainty and pain of the intermarriage phenomenon. Again and again, Reform rabbis describe this choice as one of the most difficult of their professional lives. Speaking in a sermon to his Reform congregation on *Rosh Hashanah* (1992), Rabbi James Rosenberg (R) reveals that:

> ...no professional decision which I have made during my 21 years as an ordained rabbi has caused me more personal pain than my decision not to officiate at interfaith marriages. ...

A Reform rabbi wonders whether he would have more influence on intermarried couples if he would agree to officiate, but like Rabbi Rosenberg, he nonetheless feels that doing so would be too serious a violation of Jewish tradition. In our interview with him, he told us of his torn, even tortured, feelings:

> ...I have said that any thinking rabbi on either side of this intermarriage issue should be a rabbi in anguish and I am. I somehow wish that I could do it...I am in anguish and wonder what is the right thing. If I structured something where there was follow up and integration and involvement — could I get them to have Jewish families? There is a part of me that says yes you could, and a part of me that says there is a reason why the person has chosen not to convert...I am in anguish over this. I wish there were no rabbis who did intermarriages.

Though his movement prevents him from officiating, and so on that level it is not even an issue for him, a Conservative rabbi describes privately his pain about not officiating, even while he believes quite firmly in his stance:

> I am torn in the sense that I really feel for these people. There are people that I believe really want their rabbi there. What I say to them is that not only can I not do it officially, but according to Jewish law...I have to be very careful in choosing my words — clearly a marriage between a Jew and a non-Jew is not a Jewish marriage according to Jewish law. What I say to them is that I cannot attend, I cannot officiate because this

is not according to my standards and my understanding. This is not a Jewish marriage, but it is not to say that it is not a valid marriage. I can give you my blessing and my love and still care about you, and not to say that the synagogue doesn't still welcome you. It is a hard message for people to hear.

The sort of personal anguish and worry over the potential alienation of valued congregants felt by this Conservative rabbi induce some rabbis never to mention intermarriage or the question of officiation from the pulpits at all, as we shall see below. Other rabbis, however, choose the best-attended services of the year to discuss these issues with their congregants. Usually, as with Rabbi Michael Herzbrun's *Yom Kippur* sermon (R, 1992), these talks convey feelings of angst and misgiving:

> ...From my own perspective, I believe that whether a rabbi is willing to officiate at an intermarriage or whether he chooses not to, neither choice he makes is really adequate or satisfactory. No matter which way he decides, he loses something. For one thing, I can tell you personally that it hurts to say "no" to a couple who comes to me and asks me to do the wedding. Twice, members from my own immediate family asked me if I could do the wedding, and I don't think that they really understood why I couldn't do it. So that hurt.

A Reform rabbi also adopts a policy regarding family members which very few parents, even very few rabbis, as he puts it, "have the stomach for." He went so far as to cut off communications with one daughter when she was dating a non-Jew, and threatened another daughter that if she married her non-Jewish boyfriend, he would not be permitted in the house. One can see the amount of pain his stance cost him from his obvious relief when the situations abated:

> My daughter was going with someone who was not Jewish and we had to break off communications for a while, until I

thought we could re-enter without losing face. Thank God that worked out and she married someone who is Jewish. Another daughter was dating a non-Jew and was very serious. I took a walk with her and I said, "...I tell you that you will always be my daughter and welcome in my home, but your non-Jewish husband will never be welcome in my home."...We always told them that they could not date non-Jews while they lived in our home. With each of the children we took strong stands. I don't think most families have the stomach for it.

Anguish is not the only emotion aroused in rabbis by intermarriage. Indeed, many rabbis find alarmist rhetoric in reference to intermarriage to be misguided. We turn now to a set of positive emotions which are felt by many rabbis in relation to intermarriage.

PLEASURE, POWER AND POSSIBILITY

A Sense of Possibility
Regarding Intermarriage in General

Some rabbis view the intermarriage rates with relative calm, noting that some who intermarry remain strongly connected to Judaism, and also suggesting that the ultimate value in a marriage is not whether both partners are Jewish — but whether they are compatible. In a *Rosh Hashanah* sermon (1991) largely devoted to encouraging congregants to get more involved in the spiritual aspects of Judaism, Rabbi Charles Lippman (R) asserts that the intermarriage rate is not a calamity. Indeed, he urges congregants to rejoice when their children find partners with whom they are happy:

Whether or not intermarriage is a problem depends, of course, upon one's point of view...I understand how upset many feel about intermarriage,...I empathize with distraught parents. But one of the worst consequences of intermarriage is that violent opposition to it can tear families apart. Wanting our children and grandchildren to marry Jews is fine and reasonable. Wanting them to be happy is more important.

Rabbi Raphael Asher (R) affirms the potentially positive dimensions of intermarriage even more strongly. Noting with pleasure the reaffirmation of Judaism that sometimes comes about as a result of an intermarriage, he delights in the beauty that he sees in these unions, even pronouncing them *beshert*:

> ...You have all heard the arguments that intermarriage points to assimilation which points to the disappearance of the Jewish people by the year 2000 and whatever...My own experience has shown me different, and I have taken a position with my marriage and conversion policies which does not wince with every non-Jewish bride or groom that comes before me, eager to marry their Jewish partner beneath the *chupah*.. More often than not I have witnessed the wonderful ironies which these marriages have created: an acceptance by non-Jews of Judaism as a most sensible approach to child-rearing in a secular society. A renewed interest in one's own Jewish heritage because of the challenge of intermarriage to clarify the reasons for one's devotion. The look in a couple's eyes and in the eyes of gorgeous children tells me that these marriages, too, are *beshert*, destined by God's providence.

Pride Regarding the Officiation Decision

We have seen that rabbis feel anguish with regard to their decision about officiating at intermarriage ceremonies. After the difficult decision has been made, rabbis often indicate a sense of pride and pleasure. Most rabbis who will officiate at intermarriages say again and again that they will not officiate at just any intermarriage — they officiate when certain requirements have

been met. Indeed, many rabbis find that their agreement to officiate can be a kind of incentive with which to propel intermarried
couples toward more Jewish learning and involvement. While
Chapter Three will look more deeply into the rabbis' various policies and requirements regarding couples whose marriages they
perform, for now we will focus on the rabbis' emotions around
the ceremonies they perform.

Rabbi Raphael Asher (R) has devised a six-month course of
study which aims to help both Jewish and non-Jewish partners to
become committed to being a "coguardian of a Jewish home,"
which "will better enable them to facilitate the Jewishness of the
home." Rabbi Asher feels that this course has a powerful, positive
impact:

> By the time I start under the *chupah* with the couple at the
> wedding (and I do insist upon a *chupah*), I feel quite certain
> that a Jewish home is being established with both bride and
> groom equally willing and able to facilitate its Jewish charac-
> ter. I also feel confident that such a home has as good a chance
> of enduring, or better, as one in which a conversion has tran-
> spired in deference to a wedding date.

Rabbi Asher believes so much in the process he has devised
that he considers his practice of officiating at selected intermarriages to be "officiating at the founding of a Jewish home."

In an extremely dramatic gesture, Rabbi Howard A. Berman
(R) demonstrates what he feels have been the overwhelmingly
positive results of his decision to officiate at intermarriages and to
welcome intermarried couples into his congregation. Speaking to
his entire congregation on *Rosh Hashanah* Eve (1991) and referring to the recently published reports that over 50% of American
Jews were marrying out of the faith, Berman chastises those who
would criticize his officiation at intermarriages:

> What is my answer to those who will now point to these new
> statistics and blame the problem on our young people? What

is my response to those who will point to Berman and Sinai and say, "Look at the harm you're doing"? Let me give my answer — and the response of Chicago Sinai Congregation…I am going to ask every couple here tonight that has joined this temple through our Outreach Program, or parents whose family has been supported through our position [on intermarriage] to rise — I want to show our own statistics. I want all of us to see for ourselves — the fruit of the seeds we are planting for the future. …

At this point, according to the notes in a printed edition of Rabbi Berman's sermon, "about 150 young people stood up — followed by sustained applause by the congregation." Clearly, Rabbi Berman derives joy and strength from the presence of the people he feels might have been lost to Judaism if he had not been willing to officiate at interfaith weddings. "Any thinking rabbi on either side of this intermarriage issue should be a rabbi in anguish," one Conservative rabbi stated. On the contrary, clearly some rabbis who do officiate at intermarriages enjoy great pride and pleasure, as seen in some of the other interviews.

While it would be hard to expect quite as much pleasure among those who find themselves having to say "no" all of the time, still there is nonetheless pride and empowerment among rabbis on that side as well. One source of power comes from having a sense of integrity, the sense that one does not waiver in the face of social pressure, the sense that one is connected to a long history and to a higher truth. One Reform rabbi expresses his pride in his connection to centuries of Jewish history, and his certainty about the integrity involved in maintaining the "standards" of the tradition:

I am not ashamed to say that we have standards. You may not like the standards, I may not always like the standards, but they are there and there are basic definitions that have been used for many, many centuries. One of them is who is a Jew, and one of them is what makes a marriage a Jewish marriage.

A Conservative rabbi derives pride from fulfilling a role that he could not possibly fulfill if he were to officiate at intermarriages. Refraining from doing so, he is well-situated to warn couples of potential difficulties of intermarriage, and to encourage them to rethink their decision to marry:

> ...It sounds so horrible to break up a relationship, and it can be very devastating. But I have no problem when a couple comes in thinking of intermarrying of saying right out from the beginning that you realize there are enough problems in a normal healthy marriage and you are starting off with what can be very, very serious problems. Very often conversion isn't the answer. It isn't necessarily going to solve the problems. What about the children and the non-Jewish grandparents? How are they going to feel when they can't celebrate the holidays with their grandchildren? There are all kinds of walls that can be created. I have no qualms about letting people know that [an intermarriage] is a very, very difficult situation.

If the officiation issue engenders anguish and doubt in rabbis, it clearly engenders some feelings of powerful accomplishment as well. Those rabbis who do officiate at intermarriages purport to affect the level of Jewish commitment and observance in the homes of the couples with whom they work. And those rabbis who do not officiate at intermarriages enjoy the power that comes from feeling that they are withstanding pressure, and thereby upholding sacred tradition, and helping to preserve the people.

Pleasure Regarding Intermarried Couples in the Synagogue

We turn now from the feelings surrounding officiation to what we might call the aftermath of intermarriage. What feelings do the rabbis have about the presence of non-Jews in their congregations? How do they feel toward Jews who have married non-Jews? What about the children who are born of intermarriages?

How do rabbis' attitudes toward those who are in intermarriages differ from their attitudes toward those couples in which one partner has converted? Let us begin with what is perhaps the most salient change in a rabbi's daily life since the advent of a large number of intermarriages — the regular appearance of large numbers of Jews married to non-Jews and of non-Jews themselves in the synagogue.

Many rabbis across denominational lines express excitement about the infusion of energy and spirit brought into the synagogue — the non-Jewish spouses of Jewish congregants. Again and again, rabbis report an unusual level of commitment and participation on the part of non-Jews. A Reform rabbi articulates his pleasure at this phenomenon:

> Most of the non-Jewish partners like what they see in the synagogue. They feel an attachment and an obligation to carry out the agreement [to study Judaism and bring up Jewish children]. They want to get involved and take classes. We have found that these couples only become more active in the congregation.

A Conservative rabbi who says plainly that he is "sad" about the intermarriage phenomenon, nonetheless builds on these remarks. Not only do non-Jews often make great participants in synagogue life, but they often provide the impetus for their Jewish partners to get more involved:

> ...My experience has been that when the Jewish partner encounters the Christian partner, that becomes a very teachable moment for the Jewish partner. The Christian partner ultimately says, "You want to raise the kids Jewish. What does it mean to you?" and the Jew can't articulate it. It may be a moment in which either one of them or both of them can come and examine what Judaism might mean to them...I think it is an opportunity for us.

Reiterating and building even further on these two rabbis' remarks, Rabbi Marcia Zimmerman (R, 1993) asserts that not only can non-Jews be great synagogue members, not only do they spur their Jewish partners toward more involvement, but in their sincere exploration and questioning, intermarried couples can serve as a model for other Jews, who might have become complacent in their Judaism:

> ...Often times it is precisely because the born Jewish partner is with someone not Jewish that brings them back to Judaism. Often it is the difficult questions asked by the non-Jewish partner that makes the born Jew return to study and begin regular Jewish observance. Witnessing interfaith couples work to find a harmony of religion brings out the real and important issues for religious identity, choice of religious observance and commitment that I wish all adult Jews would struggle with. ...

For these rabbis the pleasure at the participation of non-Jews arises out of the non-Jews' willingness to explore and perhaps eventually to embrace Judaism. Their excitement rests on the possibility that the intermarried couple will become more actively, thoughtfully Jewish.

Pleasure Regarding the Possible Blending of Religions

There are a few rabbis who take a leap beyond the kind of pleasure described above and see beauty in helping intermarried couples devise ways of combining Jewish and Christian practice. A Reform rabbi — who does not serve in a congregation — represents this radical view:

> ...Years ago I did a wedding, and a woman came up to me after the wedding and said, "I want to talk to you." She was married to a Catholic man, and she was Jewish. They had an eleven-month-old son, and they had been agonizing over the nam-

ing of the child. I said, "Do a *bris*/baptism." She said, "What is that?" I told her that it was a combination of both. She said, "Is that possible?" I told her that I had done it. She got so excited, she discussed it with her husband and called me the next day and they had decided to do it. They realized that neither one nor the other was satisfactory — doing both was the only solution. We had the *bris*/baptism and it had exactly the effect we wanted it to have in bringing the families together. It includes the families and unites them, and makes them feel good and not at war with each other. This gives them an option that satisfies both.

When challenged with the contention that raising a child in two religions will confuse the child, the rabbi responds:

This is a choice the child should make...Normally there is an integration [of the two religions] and sharing and respect [between the partners]...The kid under those circumstances does not get confused. There is a very strong message that is communicated to that child — a message of respect and tolerance of the other. They see how the parents respect each other's differences within the framework of love, and it works. That child is learning a powerful, powerful message that he might not have learned had he not grown up in an intermarriage.

This rabbi's view that Judaism and Christianity fit well together and that there may actually be benefits to a child growing up actively practicing two religions is an extreme one, severely criticized, as we shall see, by many of the other rabbis we studied.

Pleasure and Pride Regarding Converts and Conversion

While we will revisit the issue of conversion in another context in Chapter 3, our aim here is to explore the rabbis' feelings about it. Amidst all of the feelings of anguish and grief which

dominate rabbinic reactions to intermarriage and its consequences, the area of conversion of non-Jews to Judaism stands out
as beacon of excitement, pleasure, enthusiasm and optimism. For
most rabbis, it is probably true that a marriage involving a "Jew by
birth" and a "Jew by choice" is slightly less preferable than a marriage involving two Jews by birth. Nonetheless, rabbis of all
denominations find great joy and empowerment in their work
with converts. A Conservative rabbi's response to potential converts is more typical than he implies:

> Some of my colleagues say they don't have time for conver-
> sion. I told them they could send every one of them to me. I
> would take every one of them. I think it is the most important
> work that I do. People are hungry for something that is real
> and meaningful. The converts that we have are amazing. They
> are bright, educated, successful. This is wonderful, and that is
> what we should put our efforts into.

A Reform rabbi reiterates the thought quite directly: "Some of
the most wonderful, capable leaders in our community have
come into the Jewish world through intermarriage."

The enthusiasm for Jews by choice is sometimes overwhelming. Not only are they seen as wonderful in themselves, but the
rabbis consider them to have valuable qualities that lots of Jews by
birth lack. A Conservative rabbi sees their presence as an absolute
boon to the community:

> I love teaching conversion students who were Catholic
> because they generally have a sense of religion and a sense of
> ritual — they may not have liked it, but they went to church
> every Sunday. And they went to Catholic school for more
> years than they care to remember. If they can translate that
> ritual — that caring about ritual — to a Jewish community
> that has largely forgotten it and finds it silly, that will be one
> of the greatest gifts. There is so much that Jews by choice can
> teach native-born Jews about a love of something that they
> have found, about love of learning.

Rabbi Mark Kunis (O), writing in the *Atlanta Jewish Times*, shares the idea that conversion should be promoted, for converts enrich Jewish life:

> Current surveys show that conversionary couples (couples where one spouse is a convert) are usually *more* observant of customs and traditions than couples where both spouses are Jewish. Converts are usually more observant than their fellow Jews, because they *want* to be Jewish. I know that all of us know people who converted and weren't sincere, but the data show that this is the exception today and not the rule...
>
> ...I urge every synagogue to form a support group for intermarried couples — an idea I had previously rejected... Statistics demonstrate that the tradition of discouraging conversions and shunning intermarried couples leads only to disaster. Rather, we should look upon this as an opportunity — an opportunity to celebrate Jewish life...and an opportunity to strengthen Jewish life.
>
> Today's converts, the surveys show, welcome the standards. They want to do it right. (emphasis in original)

We have seen that rabbis' reactions to high rates of intermarriage and its ramifications are by no means monolithic. While most look upon the general phenomenon with grief, many count non-Jews or recently converted Jews among their most thoughtful and vital congregants and students. While some rabbis feel ongoing anguish regarding their officiation decision, others take pride and power from their decision — either for or against. While some rabbis see intermarriage as a calamity of proportions akin to the Holocaust, others learn from the Holocaust that intermarriage is not such a disaster. Given the depth of these competing views and emotions, it is to be expected that America's rabbis seek to argue the righteousness of the positions they take, and that they sometimes feel huge waves of anger — at other rabbis, at their congregants, even at their own family members. In the face of anger from other rabbis and from their congregants, rabbis naturally seek to defend their positions. We turn now to these twin feelings experienced commonly by rabbis with reference to intermarriage — anger and defensiveness.

ANGER AND DEFENSIVENESS

When a rabbi feels anger about the issue of intermarriage, it can be directed at any number of targets. Some of the anger may be denominational; a Reform rabbi feeling hostile about the Conservative movement or vice versa, for example. Some Conservative and Orthodox (and even Reform) rabbis believe that the Reform movement has weakened the normative stances against intermarriage and thereby undermined the rabbinate in general in the ability to limit intermarriage. This anger may be felt about the Reform movement as a whole or a specific rabbi or group of rabbis who are believed to be engaged (even if not intentionally) in the weakening of Judaism. Part of the denominational anger comes from the feeling that the expectations of the Jewish public have been altered in a major way and that the lives of rabbis who do not perform intermarriage wedding ceremonies have been made more difficult. Congregants and non-congregants alike know that *some* rabbis will officiate at an intermarriage ceremony. Rabbis feel that individuals become more indignant or demanding because the landscape has been so dramatically rearranged by the rabbis who perform intermarriages.

Anger against those who are perceived to be weakening standards derives from two separate feelings. The first feeling is that rabbis need to hold the ideological line and be the spokespeople speaking out against intermarriage, and the key proponents of the "prevention strategy." Rabbis who cross that line are perceived by some of their colleagues to be agents of destruction for the Jewish people. This anger is ideological and passionate, intertwined with the rabbis' deep sense of commitment and love for the Jewish people and the sense of tragic loss. The anger becomes stronger from a sense of collegial betrayal. When an entire denomination "allows" intermarriage, often perceived to be facilitating or even encouraging it, other denominational rabbis become hostile.

Anger can also be felt about specific rabbis. For example, non-congregation rabbis, "free-lancers" who officiate at inter-marriage weddings, are seen by some of their colleagues at best as "entrepreneurs," and at worst as communal "prostitutes." Some rabbis believe that other rabbis are assisting intermarriage wed-dings primarily for the financial gain — the fees that are earned from the task that legitimate rabbis would not facilitate. Anger may be directed toward this general class of rabbis, or to specific rabbis who are known to be the primary purveyors of intermar-riage philosophy, counseling and action.

Anger is also connected to the feeling that some rabbis have that if all their colleagues were united in their opposition to inter-marriage, then the Jewish public would have nowhere to turn, and therefore would be less demanding and hostile about rabbis who advocate stronger prevention standards. In other words, some rabbis feel that their colleagues make life harder for them by encouraging Jews to ask: "Some rabbis perform intermarriage, some welcome intermarried couples, some are more sympathet-ic, why aren't *you*?" Some rabbis believe that their colleagues are putting them in extremely awkward and difficult-to-defend posi-tions. More liberal rabbis may be angry about colleagues who do not adequately assist intermarried couples — for driving poten-tial Jews away from Judaism. If other rabbis were only more open, then the Jewish population would not be diminished by missed opportunities. Some Reform rabbis are angry because they believe that the closed-door policy drives Jews away.

Anger may also be directed at congregants, even if a rabbi feels empathy. If a congregant requests the rabbi to perform an intermarriage, attend a baby naming, or some other activity that it is known the rabbi will not sanction, rabbis can feel angry that congregants put them in the awkward position of having to reject them. This is especially troublesome when there is a close relationship between a rabbi and a congregant and the rabbi feels forced to take an action that is either unpleasant or unacceptable to the congregant. If the congregant becomes angry, this may in turn engender feelings of anger in the rabbi as well. The rabbi may feel hostile to protect himself/herself from the congregant who made a request or demand that could not be fulfilled. The rabbi may feel that the congregant unnecessarily puts them through some ritual rejection that makes everyone feel bad. While in some cases the rabbi may be empathetic, sympathetic or compassionate; in other cases they may also feel angry in the face of anger, or even in the face of someone else's pain. The rabbi's feeling of "why did you do this to me?" may result in a rift between the rabbi and the congregant.

The rabbi may feel anger toward congregational leadership. The issue of intermarriage can become an arena for lay/professional struggle. Where there is a tenuous or strained relationship between the rabbi and the lay leadership, the intermarriage issue may become one of the points of contention. Sometimes the rabbi's stance on intermarriage issues may be the source of conflict, but can also be a battleground as a proxy for other controversies. As in a troubled marriage, where any issue may become the focal point for unhappiness or discord, the issue of intermarriage serves as a good lightning rod for both lay leadership and rabbi alike to vent their unhappiness or frustration. The rabbi may be extremely angry at the congregational leadership for whatever distance is between them.

The rabbi may also feel anger at himself/herself. Because rabbis are so often ambivalent about many intermarriage issues, any action may produce embarrassment, confusion or a whole other range of emotions outlined in this chapter. These emotions may be turned inward, with a rabbi feeling angry that they are unable to do more, angry at their failure, angry that they have such a sense of responsibility, and so on. Some rabbis second-guess themselves, which can produce self-targeted anger about what they might have done or should have done.

Rabbis sometimes express anger at the seminaries that train them. They feel as if their preparation for the real world in dealing with intermarriage is inadequate. Faced with so many day-to-day decisions concerning intermarriage, they feel as if discussions, teaching and debate about the issue are lacking at the seminary. They are not taught how to approach congregants, how to deal with their own feelings, how to interact with the congregation over these issues, and so on. It reflects a more general feeling that many rabbis have that the seminaries are not adequately preparing them for contemporary congregational life in a number of ways.

The arguments posed by rabbis on both sides of the intermarriage officiation issue are surprisingly similar. Each side argues that its response is in the best interests of Jewish survival, that its response is more authentically Jewish, and that its response shows compassion to the individual couples involved. Interestingly, the officiation issue — and the anger and defensiveness around it — spills over into the thoughts and words of Conservative and Orthodox rabbis, even though they personally do not have to choose whether or not to officiate.

Anger at Other Rabbis — in the Name of Jewish Survival

Those who choose to officiate at intermarriages defend their practice with the fervent argument that they are doing what needs to be done for the continuity of the Jewish people. And they express anger at those rabbis who in their words "turn Jews away." Rabbi Marc Brownstein (R) writes in the Houston *Jewish Herald Voice* (1992) of the damage wrought by those rabbis who refuse to officiate at intermarriages:

...One wonders how many of those 75% of the children of interfaith marriages lost to Judaism were lost because the couple was turned away by one rabbi after another. Sanctions are not the answer. Turning the couple away leaves a permanent scar on the psyche of the Jew, and by implication degrades the person of the non-Jew. All the niceties of theological principles and religious exclusiveness, and all of the protestations of love by the rabbi turning them away, cannot salve over the rejection and the hurt.

Rabbi Howard Berman (R) similarly defends his decision to officiate at intermarriages, and lambastes those who do not officiate, asserting that his "ultimate priority" — the survival of the Jewish people — hangs in the balance. Though early in his career he refused to officiate at intermarriages, Rabbi Berman came to see this refusal as irresponsible, even "pathetically futile" (1991):

...Either we could rant and rave and "sit *shivah*," [a week of mourning after a death] as generations had done before; either I as a rabbi could reject such couples and refuse to support them; or I and my congregation could warmly welcome them — celebrate their weddings — work with them, and help them find a home together in Judaism. I came to believe that the bitterness and alienation that many young Jews felt, because of the ways their parents and rabbis responded to their relationships, was tantamount to creating a self-fulfilling prophecy. Intermarriage would indeed mean the end of the Jewish faith and people — if we rejected and turned these young people away!...

...Friends — there is no question that this latest development [the 1990 Population Study] in the complex controversy of intermarriage in the Jewish community is going to cause intensified debate. The hard-liners in the rabbinate — Orthodox and Reform — will retrench in their opposition to officiating at these wedding ceremonies...and will do everything they can to try to coerce young Jews to marry only other Jews — a pathetically futile, totally unrealistic and illusive effort. ...

One can hardly miss the combative tone of Rabbi Berman's words. The word "retrench" connotes that there is indeed a war going on; the use of the word "coerce" implies that the other side enlists anti-democratic, even tyrannical methods to enforce its will.

Rabbi Samuel Silver (R), who has written a book on his experience officiating at intermarriages (1977), draws support for his work from "the other side" itself. (This work was completed before the current "crisis.") Even Orthodox Jews, he contends, come to recognize that his approach is the one with the best chance of keeping the most Jews Jewish:

> ...I have performed weddings for the offspring of traditional rabbis and for the children of officials of Orthodox synagogues. In almost every case, the parents have thanked me profusely for what I did, declaring that the Jewish ceremony I provided gave the families a "fighting chance" to keep the young couple involved within the ambiance of Jewish life.

If the strongest opponents of intermarriage send their sons and daughters to a rabbi who performs intermarriage, surely that rabbi is doing right by Jews and Judaism.

On the other hand, the level of disdain for rabbis who perform intermarriages as mercenaries can be high. Silver goes on to say:

> ...the demand of a Jewish ceremony for mixed couples has continued unabated. So persistent is this demand that there has, lamentably, arisen a cluster of free-lance rabbis and cantors who are commercializing the enterprise...In fact, some of us intermarriers have been lumped with this coterie and we are often accused of doing what we do for monetary reasons. Occasionally when someone asks me, "What is your fee?" and I give my standard response, "Nothing," there's a gasp of incredulity.

Rabbis who do not officiate would not concede the point so quickly. They contend that *their* approach is the one with the "fighting chance" of encouraging Jews to live Jewish lives. They express anger at the rabbis who do perform intermarriages. Here is how the argument runs: Though a couple might approach a rabbi hoping that the rabbi will officiate at their wedding, the rabbi's refusal may in fact draw the couple toward Judaism. For, as these rabbis contend, people grow to respect a rabbi who has limits and to honor a religion in which "not just everything goes." Recalling a man who spoke to him after he had refused to officiate at his wedding, a Reform rabbi says, "he was so glad that I didn't do it because now he has such great respect for his Jewishness." The rabbi explains:

> ...A lot of my colleagues think that by officiating at mixed-marriages we retain some of the people who otherwise we would lose. I think that is also an illusion because I have used a totally different approach and have retained the friendship of almost every one of those people and they have all gravitated toward Judaism. They see the solid integrity in my approach.

Rabbi Michael Zedek (R) refuses to officiate at intermarriages, but strongly encourages the non-Jewish partner to consider conversion. In his 1992 *Yom Kippur* sermon, he quotes from a letter he received from a someone at whose wedding he had refused to officiate:

> ...If you had performed intermarriages, I would never have had this chance to learn...to experience...I probably would never have chosen the path of conversion, because I would have had no idea what Judaism was. But now my life is changed and for all time...

Where Brownstein, Berman and Silver underscore the rightness of their decision to officiate, others including Zedek defend the integrity — and the efficacy — of their refusal. What could be better validation for the practice of *not* officiating, indeed, than a recommendation of that practice from someone who has been refused? And so it is that both "officiators" and "non-officiators" claim the high ground of promoting Jewish survival. But that is not their only defense.

Defending the Officiation Decision — in View of the Holocaust

Perhaps the ultimate defense of any stand on an issue affecting the contemporary Jewish world is the claim that one has the lessons of recent Jewish history on one's side. Earlier, we saw the Holocaust evoked in a grief-stricken analogy to the kind of decimation that intermarriage might wreak on the Jewish people. Rabbis on both sides of the officiation issue enlist the Holocaust, too, to defend their actions on the basis of the beliefs of Holocaust survivors. Here, a Reform rabbi tells of an encounter with a survivor nearly thirty years ago, when he had just started officiating at intermarriages and giving speeches on the subject:

> ...I got called to give a talk to B'nai B'rith in San Francisco, in 1968. They had the largest group they had ever had. You could have heard a pin drop — people listened. When it was over, people got up and walked to the other two speakers — I was boycotted. As I got to the door, there was this woman who was about five feet tall and she said, "I lost all my family in Europe, and I want you to know that you are right and they are wrong. Don't stop."

Compare this Reform rabbi's defense of his practice — in the name of the dead and of the survivors — with the argument of a Conservative rabbi, who objects to intermarriage on these same grounds. Recognizing the potential offense caused by comparing the mass murder of Jews with a personal choice to marry a non-Jew, the Conservative rabbi justifies his use of that metaphor:

> ...A number of people challenged me on the use of the word Holocaust in relationship to the disappearance of Jews through intermarriage. I want people to know that I got permission to use that term from a Holocaust survivor. I know that Holocaust survivors feel that is what is going on regarding intermarriage — they use that word to describe it all the time. They have told me countless times that they see the intermarriage picture in America of what Hitler tried to do and couldn't. I would never make that comparison if I didn't hear it all the time from survivors themselves.

Rabbis on both sides of the officiation issue claim that the interests of the survival of the Jewish people are on their side; they both have Holocaust survivors who agree with them. According to one line of thought, the Holocaust should have taught us acceptance; we should have learned to welcome the stranger into our midst. According to a more prevalent line of thought, the Holocaust should have taught us the fragility of the Jewish people's survival; we must not give way to assimilation. Rabbis on either side of the issue feel genuine wrath at the others — and their evoking the Holocaust in this context betrays just how heated this disagreement can be.

Anger at Other Rabbis —
in the Name of Jewish Authenticity

The Holocaust is not the only flashpoint for rabbis' anger at one another with regard to intermarriage. They also argue, and feel anger at other rabbis — in the name of Jewish authenticity. Rabbis who do officiate at intermarriages are particularly vulnerable to the challenge that their action lacks validity from the standpoint of Judaism. Facing that challenge, Rabbi Bruce Kahn (R, 1981), almost twenty years ago, acknowledges that his decision violates *Talmud* and *Midrash*, but proclaims that it adheres to Torah and God's law:

I perform intermarriages...I claim before you that I do not violate Torah or God's law when I marry a Jew and a non-Jew. What I do violate is the *Talmudic* and *Midrashic* understanding of Torah, understandings written 1500 to 2000 years after Abraham, Isaac, Jacob and Moses lived.

A Reform rabbi, too, finds inspiration for his unabashed pleasure at officiating at marriages between Jews and non-Jews in his reading of Jewish prophetic texts:

My agenda is not to make more Jews, my agenda is to help create a world where intolerance, hatred and violence...are gone. The purpose of Judaism, if we look at the teachings of the prophets — Isaiah, Jeremiah, Micah and even the rabbis in the early period — their purpose was not to make more Jews. Their purpose was to spread the message that most people of good will would embrace today anyway. If Judaism has any goal at all, it is to convey this message.

Judaism, this rabbi argues, teaches the necessity of working towards a world of tolerance and peace. Good people of all faiths believe in these things, too. Why not, then, argues this rabbi, permit the marriage of like minds?

We have seen that rabbis who decline to officiate at intermarriages often feel torment about their decision; they feel torn between compassion for the couple and respect for Jewish tradition. Indeed, rabbis who do officiate at intermarriages often claim that the dictates of tradition and the impulses of compassion are one and the same — and both demand that rabbis agree to officiate. Rabbi Marc Brownstein (R) explains:

To embrace the Jew and non-Jew, rather than turn them away as they seek to be married...is the only choice consistent to that which is fundamental to Judaism. The concept of the unity of humankind is intrinsic to Jewish tradition. It is as Solomon prayed at the dedication of the Temple in Jerusalem: "My house shall be a house of prayer for all people." Have we not been taught that "the stranger shall be unto you as the home born"? Do we not insist that we all have been created in the image of God? Shall this fundamental principle be cast aside to embrace some spurious notion of tribal purity? Rabbis should officiate at interfaith marriages, and the synagogues should embrace interfaith couples. ...

Clearly Brownstein uses fighting words here as he refers to "some spurious notion of tribal purity." No wonder, then, that arguments such as those of Brownstein — claiming the sanction of Torah and tradition for officiating at intermarriages — evoke unabashed wrath from many of their rabbinic colleagues. An Orthodox rabbi, referring to rabbis who officiate at intermarriages, admonishes:

...They are perpetrating a fraud. It is not a Jewish marriage. You can't perform a Jewish marriage if both parties are not Jewish. I think it is better for them to get married by a Justice of the Peace...

Another Orthodox rabbi phrases his disgust even more strongly:

I think they [rabbis who perform intermarriages] are ghouls because they are presiding over the death of the Jewish people. They are benefiting from it. All they are doing is showing them that Judaism is willing to prostitute itself for the sake of whatever it is that they are saying that it might be. I think you should call a spade a spade. When someone dies you don't prop them up and make believe that they are still alive.

Performing a Jewish wedding for a mixed couple is a sham, according to this point of view. It is indecent, untruthful, perhaps even criminal.

Not only Orthodox rabbis take this view of the actions of rabbis who choose to officiate at intermarriages. A Conservative rabbi sounds very much like his Orthodox colleagues:

I am very concerned about rabbis who officiate. They are creating a fraudulent ceremony and I think that is wrong. Some rabbis have no integrity at all. They would marry a fish with a goat — for whatever money they can get.

Rabbis who officiate at mixed-marriages are clearly suspect in other rabbis' eyes — some of them, indeed, are seen to be unscrupulous mercenaries.

Though his rhetoric is slightly softer, a Reform rabbi expresses scorn for colleagues of his own movement similar to that of the rabbis from the other movements:

I feel that a rabbi who officiates at mixed-marriages is doing a disservice not only to the couple but also to the Jewish community. Those rabbis that say that they are doing it for the sake of Judaism will only do it if the price is right.

Clearly, these rabbis who do not officiate feel wrath and contempt for those who do. But why should they care so much? How do the actions of other rabbis affect them? A Conservative rabbi explains how what other rabbis decide to do affects him. Their decision, he explains, impinges on him and his work:

I think that people don't understand that when a rabbi performs an intermarriage — he is attacking that institution — he is diminishing that institution. They are reducing it to something else. What they want to do is their business, but the anger comes from how they diminish Judaism for those who are still trying to preserve it...I feel that we have to present a united front against intermarriage...I am angry with the guys for breaching the wall, but I am also angry with them for legitimizing a diminished Judaism. It makes my job so

much harder...it makes it difficult for me to maintain my
position. That makes me angry. It makes me angry because
there is no legitimate Jewish tradition that he is drawing
from. ...

We see in this rabbi's response the two main sources of contention against rabbis who do officiate at intermarriages. First, in
this view, there is no basis in the tradition for performing intermarriages. Second, the existence of rabbis who say "yes" to mixed-
marriages creates tremendous pressure on those who say "no."
This view is not unanimous; some rabbis of all denominations
express respect for the decision of some of their colleagues to officiate at intermarriages.

However, we must note that rabbis are not the only focus
for the anger of other rabbis. Jewish parents who do not bring up
their children in such a way that they value Judaism as an integral
part of their lives draw anger from rabbis — for why would a
child who is not deeply rooted in Judaism choose to seek only a
Jewish spouse? Intermarried couples also draw some ire. Though
it is common, as we have seen, for rabbis to express pleasure at
their relationships with intermarried couples and at non-Jews'
willingness to learn about Judaism and to participate in synagogue life, a certain set of intermarried couples infuriates some
rabbis. We turn to these two additional sources of rabbinic pain
and displeasure.

Anger at Parents

Anger against parents is widespread. This is particularly true
among Orthodox rabbis. The abandonment of rituals and ways of
life such as *kashrut*, they believe, are fundamental to the loss of
Jewish identity and cohesiveness and directly responsible for the
intermarriage of the next generation. An Orthodox rabbi
describes what he finds to be hypocritical behavior on the part of
Jewish parents:

...I find, in general, a lot of families of intermarried are very hypocritical. The parents of the boy or girl come in screaming and yelling when they find out that their son or daughter is going to intermarry. They did not afford a decent education to these children; they did not in any way show that it was important to be Jewish — their lifestyle was hypocritically Jewish. There was nothing Jewish in their home except perhaps a bible which was a wedding present. Then all of a sudden they start screaming and yelling.

They do it also because they are embarrassed in front of their parents and grandparents. It isn't real, and the kids know that it isn't real because they are not stupid. They are Jewishly ignorant, but they are not stupid. They know that their parents never made any Jewish commitments — they never had a kosher home. A kosher home is a certain statement that you are making that you are going to discipline yourself in this way. They make an appearance on the holidays, but there was nothing beyond that. I don't think these parents have any right to scream and yell.

The prevalence of intermarriage can be blamed, in this view, on the parents not having taken a more active role in the Jewish education of their children. The adult children of Jewish parents, now on the road to intermarriage, are seen as victims of parents' lack of interest, lack of commitment, and lack of action. They are not the only children who are seen as victims.

Anger at the Actions of Intermarried Couples

We have seen the different emotions with which rabbis greet intermarried couples and non-Jewish partners — as in the case of the officiation decision, they feel everything from delight to anxiety, from empowered to apologetic. A more pointed set of emotions emerges when the children of intermarried couples are involved. Perhaps the most vehement language used to address any part of the intermarriage discussion comes up with regard to parents who bring up their children in two religions. Most rabbis see this as reprehensible.

Rabbi Richard Birnholz (R), for example, does officiate at intermarriages under some circumstances. He nonetheless reserves special disdain for those young couples who plan to bring up children in two faiths. His article, published in *Jewish Post and Opinion*, merits citation at some length, as he spells out what he calls the "abusive" nature of this two-religion arrangement:

> ...The compromise [of bringing up the children in both religions] sounds eminently reasonable. No one can argue with it, and best of all, neither parent has won or lost. Neither parent has to answer to angry grandparents on either side and neither has given up an inch of turf. And better still, both have relieved themselves of a major problem by shifting it to their child. Now the decision is no longer theirs — it's the child's...
>
> ...The parents, of course, do not see it as a problem because they do not stop to think what it is like to try to believe in Jesus as Messiah and not believe in Jesus as Messiah at the same time. Neither of them could be both Jewish and Christian at the same time, and neither thinks enough of the other's religion to convert to it, but their child is a wonder being. Their child should be able to do what they can't. Their child should be able to be Jewish today, Christian tomorrow, and the same combination of the two the next day. And the child, as you can imagine, learns to cope in a sad and painful way. In order not to hurt Mom or Dad, he dutifully follows each other's rituals and celebrates their holidays without feeling anything. Mom and Dad do not know of this religious numbness because they assume that their child is feeling both equally, and as long as there is equal representation, they are satisfied.
>
> ...Yet, how could a person, young or old, feel equally grounded in Judaism and Christianity...It's not possible emotionally or intellectually. But the parents do not consider this. As long as each's [sic] turf is protected, they are content. ...

Birnholz goes on to argue that a child brought up in two religions usually ends up religionless, because to choose a religion would be to choose between parents. Confused and burdened, torn between parents, robbed of the richness that any one religion might be able to bring, a child brought up in two religions suffers from his/her parents' inability to come to a decision. Such parenting receives Birnholz's outrage.

A Reform rabbi echoes Birnholz and many other rabbis when he says that if the children cannot be wholly Jewish, it would be far better for them to adopt another faith rather than to try to be both:

> ...Some families will send their children to the synagogue one year and the church the next, because they want to expose the children to both traditions. Bull! I have said to people better you should bring your child up as a Catholic. If I can't have them, better your child should have one tradition with an awareness that there is a Jewish heritage. Don't confuse the child or put him into a contest to please Mommy on Sunday and Daddy on Saturday. I am in anguish over this.

We understand from these passages that even though a rabbi might officiate at an intermarriage, in almost all cases the rabbi assumes that the couple will let go of the non-Jewish partner's religion, and lead a Jewish life. In Chapter 3, we will examine the specific stipulations rabbis have in this regard. But the point here is that the intermarriage issue becomes particularly loaded for many rabbis by the recognition that some families will try to combine what the rabbis feel are irreconcilable world views — those of Judaism and Christianity. If intermarriage means combining religions, most rabbis are dead-set against it — the very idea, as Fisher says, is "bull," and evokes anguish.

Some rabbis feel that if someone is serious about Judaism they would not intermarry. Because rabbis often see Judaism as an integrated whole in a person's identity and behavior, they can only conclude that others would see it as well. Therefore they reach the conclusion that someone who intermarries is not interested in Judaism, or as stated by a Conservative rabbi:

> ...for anybody who takes Judaism seriously they have to know how important Judaism in their life is outside of the synagogue. Therefore, it leads me to conclude that someone who would intermarry would probably not have a strong sense as to the importance of Judaism in the whole sphere in their life. They never experienced it on that level to know that it is that important.

Thus far we have shown how rabbis on both sides of the officiation divide take umbrage at their colleagues' behavior, and how the rabbis seek to defend their own stances in the name of Jewish survival, Jewish authenticity and the Holocaust. We have also provided examples of rabbinic indignation toward the actions of some intermarried couples. But perhaps more prevalent even than anger and defensiveness in the emotional kaleidoscope experienced by rabbis around the intermarriage issue are feelings of anxiety, frustration and powerlessness. Rabbis who oppose intermarriage, for example, may be seen even by loyal congregants as lacking compassion — and this is likely to leave the rabbi feeling anxious, frustrated and misunderstood. Rabbis who oppose intermarriage may nonetheless want to welcome intermarried couples into their congregations, and negotiating both of those impulses may cause anxiety. Opposing intermarriage in communities where everyone seems to be intermarrying may induce a sense of powerlessness. We turn, now, to this set of emotions and the conditions that evoke them.

POWERLESSNESS, ANXIETY, FRUSTRATION

Powerlessness and Resignation

Rabbis often feel a sense of powerlessness in confronting the issue of intermarriage. For some, the powerlessness comes from a feeling that they are constrained by their denominational structure. Some who disagree with their denomination's approach to intermarriage feel that they are powerless to act. For example, Conservative rabbis may feel that they are willing to perform interfaith marriages under certain conditions but cannot remain within the fold of the Conservative movement and engage in this activity. Others, particularly Reform rabbis who personally oppose outreach strategies, feel powerless in the face of so many congregational demands that they "give in" to the prevailing culture.

The feeling of powerlessness is often a response to the overwhelming demographic realities of contemporary Jewish life. Some rabbis feel that no matter what they personally do in terms of addressing the intermarriage issue that they cannot have a significant or substantial effect on the overall future of Jewish life. The sea-change of assimilation is so dramatic that many rabbis feel that they are swimming upstream, unable to adequately influence the future of Jewish life through their actions.

On the other hand, some rabbis feel a sense of empowerment by refusing to perform intermarriages. In the tremendous convergence of trends toward more assimilation, some rabbis feel that they are "holding the line" and through their individual actions exert some positive influence. For some, any act allows them to feel as if they are doing *something*, and that refusing to perform intermarriages or taking other actions that uphold standards gives them a sense of control in an otherwise out-of-control situation.

Along with the feeling of empowerment comes a feeling of righteousness. Even if they individually cannot stem the tide of assimilation, by acting correctly and behaving in a morally defensible way they feel that they are not personally contributing to the decline of Jewish life. Some rabbis take the opposite view. They feel empowered through performing intermarriages and being more welcoming to the participation of non-Jews in congregational and Jewish life in general. They feel that by reaching out and addressing the problem with practical approaches, they are responding to the changes in the Jewish world (rather than ignoring them) and are actively preserving and enriching Jewish life. They feel that they are powerless to prevent intermarriage and therefore can assert their influence most by integrating the intermarried couples into Jewish life. Some also believe that by reaching out to intermarried couples they may integrate future generations of intermarried couples into Jewish life. This provides rabbis with a feeling of accomplishment, doing something positive as opposed to being passive observers to assimilation. It is interesting that rabbis can feel both powerless and powerful regardless of which actions they take.

Powerlessness is coupled with resignation, a feeling of "there is nothing we can do about intermarriage and we are doomed." While some who are resigned to the fact of intermarriage believe that the Jewish community can recover through outreach and integration, others believe that high levels of intermarriage are inevitable. The resignation is more focused on outcomes: Large numbers of Jews will marry non-Jews, there is no redemption, and the Jewish people will disappear or diminish.

Anxiety of the Tightrope —
Balancing Acceptance and Rejection

As many rabbis who do not officiate at intermarriages put it, they have to find a way to "discourage intermarriage while embracing the intermarried." No wonder that trying to discourage and embrace at the same time should cause some anxiety; this is a difficult line to navigate. In a sermon (1994), Rabbi Dennis Ross (R) describes quite openly the tightrope on which he finds himself, and the worry it causes him:

>...This morning, I have to call for Jewish survival on the one hand as I try to reach out to the intermarried and the parents

of the intermarried with compassion on the other hand. Then I worry that, no matter how carefully I have researched my topic or how well I may express myself, you might leave this sanctuary with the wrong impression. If I speak about the difficulty of making an intermarriage work, you might conclude that all intermarriages are likely to end in divorce — and that's not true. If I describe the makings of the many successful intermarriages, you might think I am giving your children a green light to go ahead and do it, which I do not want to do. Above all, my raising the issues of interfaith dating and intermarriage this morning will put some of you on the spot — and that's certainly not my goal. ...

Rabbi Rifat Sonsino (R) continues these themes in a sermon (1991) in which he compares himself to Tevye of *Fiddler on the Roof*. Tevye, of course, understands the unstable fiddler as a metaphor for his own shaky existence. Such is the balancing act of rabbis, who like Sonsino, strive to communicate caring while retaining their sense of Jewish authenticity:

I have chosen not to perform interfaith marriages, because when I officiate at a Jewish wedding I do not only bless the couple, but declare that the marriage is a Jewish marriage, during which bride and groom proclaim their loyalty to the covenant of Sinai by saying, "By means of this ring I take you as my wife/husband according to the faith of Israel." However, I feel for those who for one reason or another have decided to marry outside of the faith. I counsel them. I am available to them and their parents. I have created and continue to support the Outreach Program in our Temple. I walk a very thin line between my conscience and my care and concern for the people I deal with. ...

Walking "a very thin line," rabbis often have to be particularly alert about what they say to whom, and when. The demand for such caution creates anxiety of its own.

The Anxiety of Watching One's Words

Despite the sort of enthusiasm cited earlier for the strength brought to the Jewish community by intermarried couples, many rabbis feel constrained by their presence as well. One of the most frequently cited problems is that because there are already so many intermarried couples present, it is hard for rabbis to speak their minds on the issue of intermarriage. A Conservative rabbi indicates his frustration:

> ...One of my congregants said to me, "As a member of the membership committee I would ask you please — no matter what you say you are going to alienate somebody — so please don't mention it [intermarriage]." But I don't think that is right — I don't believe in censure of the pulpit.

Quite pointedly choosing not to broach the topic from the pulpit, but to write in his synagogue's newsletter where he can "explore it in greater depth," Rabbi Howard Gorin (C) begins a series of articles on his approach to intermarriage with the following story of an exchange with a congregant:

> "Rabbi [the congregant said], you have always counseled us that when we have a criticism of what you have done, we should share it with you directly. I couldn't let the New Year begin without letting you know that what you said last year about intermarriage was like rubbing salt in our wounds."
> I have been reticent about speaking on this topic ever since, and I cringe whenever I learn from colleagues that they will be speaking about intermarriage in a High Holiday sermon. ...

Speaking out against intermarriage will inevitably be perceived by many congregants as rubbing salt in their wounds and downright offensive. To avoid inflicting such pain or arousing the anger of valued congregants, many rabbis refrain entirely from preaching on the subject. Rabbi Howard Greenstein (R) wrote to us explaining that while he has held panel discussions on the sub-ject at *Oneg Shabbat*, he had no sermons to share on the topic of intermarriage. In fact, he contends, "it's a serious mistake to preach on this subject, precisely because it is so volatile and dis-tressful." He goes on to say:

> ...No matter how delicately or sensitively a rabbi may treat the subject, invariably people will hear it on the basis of their deeply-held and preconceived convictions. I don't know of any colleague who has ever spoken on this issue from the pul-pit who has not aroused a storm of protest, however balanced he/she believes his/her view might be.

Storm-inducing or not, many rabbis do, as we have seen, choose to speak about intermarriage from the pulpit. We received a surprising number of sermons delivered on High Holidays, per-haps the services during the year most likely to attract intermar-ried couples. But even when rabbis do speak about intermarriage during a sermon, their discomfort, their worry that they will be misunderstood and their fear of alienating some of their congre-gation is palpable. Rabbis are in general good talkers, and speak from a position of authority. And yet the tentativeness and hesi-tation with which they speak on this topic could not be more pro-nounced. The following are a sampling of a number of the pre- or post-sermon apologies which the rabbis delivered.

Rabbi Larry Mahrer (R) ends a sermon that urges parents to discuss their disapproval of intermarriage with their young chil-dren, and that advises college-age youth to go to colleges with an active Jewish life with this signature statement:

> ...This was not a pleasant sermon to deliver tonight. I was not very comfortable doing it. My guess is that some of you were not comfortable listening to these words. If that is the case, please understand that was not my intention. My goal was to be as positive as possible about a negative subject.

Rabbi Daniel Pernick (R), similarly trying "to be as positive as possible," delivers a long, half-humorous preface to his sermon. The introduction emphasizes the rabbi's apprehension that he will be prejudged and misunderstood:

> "I know you believe you understand what you think I said, but I am not sure you realize that what you heard is not what I meant."
>
> This confusing statement is a crucial preface to any sermon dealing with the subject of intermarriage. For as soon as some people hear the terms "intermarriage," "mixed-marriage," or "interfaith marriage," they have already decided both what the rabbi will say and what their reaction will be. ...

Those like Rabbi Pernick feel they must speak out about an issue as pertinent as intermarriage because they must do what they can, but they clearly do it without total confidence that their words will be heard or heeded.

Like Pernick, Rabbi Donald Rossoff (R) tries to get a laugh while he broaches the subject, anxious not to be misunderstood or tuned out:

> ...What we learned, friends [from the 1990 Jewish Population Survey], was that as persons we are integrally part of the American agenda of life, liberty and the pursuit of happiness and that as a people, we're hemorrhaging. And so, as difficult as it is, it's time we talked about intermarriage.
>
> At this point, I know many of you are thinking, "Oh no. He's going to talk about me and about my parents, or my children or the person sitting next to me." I want to reassure you from the start that if you are afraid that I am going to talk about you, don't worry, I am. I am speaking about you and you and the person next to you and in front of you and in back of you. I'm speaking about you and I'm speaking about me. For in some way, intermarriage touches all of us. ...This is not easy to talk about from the pulpit. Regardless of what I

say, I run the risk of not being heard or understood, for often people hear what they expect to hear, not what is said in its entirety. ...

"I run the risk of not being understood" — this is perhaps the most common refrain we heard from rabbis, the overwhelming majority of whom felt it is appropriate for them to discourage intermarriage, but who have a hard time finding words which their congregants would listen to.

Conservative rabbis generally have as difficult a time as Reform colleagues bringing up the subject in a sermon. Rabbi Andrew Warmflash (C) expresses his uncertainty about the efficacy of his speech, groping for a way to begin, apologizing in advance to those who will feel judged:

> ...I thought for a long time before speaking about this subject here tonight. I am well aware that a significant number of families in our community are mixed-marriages. I am not here to point fingers at people or to judge them. The last thing I want to do is to make them feel uncomfortable in our congregation. Still I feel strongly that this is an issue that we must confront. ...

Rabbi Jack Segal (C) takes a unique approach to the problem of whether or not to sermonize on intermarriage. Instead of writing a sermon for all to hear, he chooses to address his message only to those he feels are the most appropriate audience. In a letter directed to college students from his congregation, he explains that his words are meant specially for them:

> ...It [interdating and intermarriage] is an extremely delicate issue and that is why I have refrained from speaking about it from the pulpit. Every week we have intermarried people in our congregation and I would not want to emotionally hurt them — and they are not the people to whom I want to address this subject. With them, the sermon is too late. This

subject, I believe, must be addressed to two groups: our college students and the parents of our young children.

Rabbi Segal recommends addressing an anti-intermarriage message to college-age students and to the parents of young children.

Just as the presence of adult married couples affects the sorts of sermons rabbis feel comfortable giving, the presence of the children of intermarried couples affects the life of the religious school. There, too, rabbis watch their words. A Reform rabbi explains, revealing a certain level of frustration:

> You would like to be able to talk about the value of Jewish marriage and Jewish family, and yet you have to be aware that there are a couple of kids who come from a family where one parent is not Jewish and so on. You've got to be very careful because the point is not to undermine the love and respect that people have for their families. How do you talk about Jewish marriage and the value of Jewish marriage when you are feeling that at times you have to tip-toe around and apologize and explain that you are not trying to insult anybody? And why should a kid who has a very strong Jewish identity think that there is something wrong with marrying a non-Jew if that is what their mother or father did?...That's what makes it so darn complicated...There are some jokes that you can't tell.

As he suggests, the rabbis feel themselves censoring their speech on at least three levels. First, it seems gravely insensitive to imply, even remotely, to a child that there is something seriously flawed with his or her parents' marriage. Second, the fact is that the children in the religious school are the children of the parents who are bringing them up to be Jewish — they are the exceptions; they are the involved ones; they are not the majority of intermarried families who have no affiliation with organized religion.

The third concern is perhaps the most trivial, but it underscores the change in ambiance the synagogues are undergoing.

Where the synagogue once was quite simply a Jewish place, filled with Jews, it's now a much more multi-cultural place. And just as women hold might back on telling certain jokes when men are around, and vice-versa, the rabbis feel a constraint that comes when any tightly-knit group or minority group is visited by out-siders — you cannot tell jokes that might offend the outsiders. In a word, the outsiders have become insiders — but the transition causes some discomfort.

Frustration at Needing to Protect the Gates

Some rabbis find it difficult to promote the value of Jewish marriage in a context of a religious school where many of the children have a non-Jewish parent. But the conflicts involving the children of intermarried couples do not end with religious school, nor are they limited to congregations with a high percentage of intermarried couples. In 1983, the Reform movement decided to accept as Jews those with a Jewish father and a non-Jewish mother, under certain conditions. Patrilineal descent was an attempt to find new approaches to dealing with the growing number of children who are raised as Jews, even if their non-Jewish mothers did not convert to Judaism. Rabbis from the other movements find themselves in the unhappy situation of having to let those "patrilineal Jews" know that by their *halachic* standards, they are not really Jews. This leaves these rabbis feeling frustrated and put upon.

A Conservative rabbi explains what has happened when he has been asked to marry a woman from his synagogue with a man who grew up considering himself fully Jewish under the patrilineal descent decision of the Reform movement:

> ...Here is somebody who is 25 years old, has grown up active in a Temple somewhere, and I am the person who is left to say, "I can't marry you unless you convert."...That is a real

tough thing to hear when you are 25 years old and have grown up and perhaps were president of your Temple's youth group, and you were active in camp. I am put in the position of being a bad guy.

This Conservative rabbi has to abide by *halachic* standards, and cannot accept as Jewish a man whose mother was not Jewish. But playing the "bad guy," guarding the gates in this way is no fun, and he is frustrated at his Reform colleagues for putting him in that position.

An Orthodox rabbi, too, finds the patrilineal descent decision to be divisive. It has forced him to be particularly wary around young members of Reform synagogue youth groups:

If I want to have all the youth groups in my community get together for event...I am going to expose my teens to a lot of children who are not *halachically* Jewish.

It is a sorry state, this comment implies, when a Jewish youth group cannot meet socially with another Jewish youth group, for fear that group will be full of non-Jews. But this rabbi is anxious to protect the teenagers in his congregation from the sticky situation of dating a Jew who is not, by his standards, really a Jew.

Powerlessness and Resignation

The Orthodox rabbi's gesture of keeping his youth group away from other denominations' youth groups indicates how much rabbis would like to be able to do something to prevent the rise of intermarriage. Some rabbis believe they ought to be able to do more, even though they intellectually understand that there are major forces in Jewish life contributing to higher rates of intermarriage. They feel a sense of responsibility and therefore guilt at their own powerlessness. Expectations run high for what rabbis can and cannot do in terms of their role and influence in the Jewish community. Some of those expectations are established by the community and others are self-imposed. The failure to effectively halt high levels of intermarriage or disintegration of Jewish families through intermarriage can make rabbis feel guilty; they ought to do something more or they ought to do something different. But when the rabbis don't know what to do differently, a sense of resignation sets in.

Resignation about intermarriage can be expressed in two different ways. The first is a feeling of resignation that no matter what preventive measures are taken, Jews will marry non-Jews. This form of resignation was stated in a sermon by Rabbi Samuel Stahl (R) of San Antonio, Texas in 1991:

> The reality is that, with our open society, we will be able to do little to stop intermarriage. What we must do is reach out to intermarried families and try to win the family to Judaism, to become part of the Jewish people. Such is the reason we have and that we vigorously support the Outreach Committee at Temple Beth El.

Stahl's resignation is about intermarriage as a phenomenon, not about the outcome — he holds out hope that non-Jewish spouses will become Jewish.

Another form of resignation is demonstrated by a Conservative rabbi when he states:

> I think that marriage between Jews and Christians in this country is just a fact of life. I think talking about preventing intermarriage is hopeful at best, and not completely realistic. I don't believe that intermarriage can be prevented. I think you can do a lot to give people good Jewish identities, but you can't prevent intermarriage. Intermarriage goes far, far beyond just a question of bad Jews marrying good Christians. I really see it as a symptom of what Jewish life is about.

Part of this feeling about intermarriage by rabbis comes from the universalism and liberalism that they believe parents teach their children. They believe that parents cannot differentiate between promoting liberalism and equality and the failure to differentiate Judaism as a distinctive religion or community. As another Conservative rabbi says:

> ...We can't do anything about it [intermarriage]. We give our children mixed-messages. We say go out into the world — everyone is equal, everyone is good. Go out to the university and whatever, but don't marry someone who is not Jewish. There is a contradiction to that. There is nothing you can say.

Some rabbis blame the low quality of Jewish education, both institutional and familial, as the root cause of intermarriage. They believe that since young Jews do not have a sense of history, tradition and knowledge of Judaism, there is no reason for them not to intermarry. Because the individual sees no difference between Jewish life and non-Jewish life from lack of learning, intermarriage is a logical outcome. An Orthodox rabbi explains this phenomenon as he sees it:

> A person grows up without any Jewish education — I'm not talking about learning a few things so that you can be *bar mitzvahed* — and lives the same lifestyle as a non-Jew. Why shouldn't the person marry a non-Jew? They don't know our traditions or what they mean. They don't understand that the Jewish people were literate when the Western world was not literate — they don't know that. They get up and eat ham and eggs on Sunday. They have a Christmas tree in the house and they don't understand. They copy the Christians' symbols. Christmas is one of two of the most holy days on the Christian calendar and it is not respectful. But to the person growing up, they don't understand these things, so why should they marry a Jew? They really don't have any Jewish identity.

Some rabbis go on to say — and this is a source of their own sense of powerlessness — that institutions cannot substitute for the family. While a formal Jewish education is critical, many rabbis argue, values are still inculcated primarily through the home and through the overall Jewish behavior of the family. Even day schools are not seen as the panacea by rabbis, if the parents are disinterested or uncooperative. Another Orthodox rabbi affirms the centrality of the parents' role:

> A lot of the kids in the Jewish day schools come from rotten homes (Jewishly speaking). They might be lovely people, but Jewishly speaking they are ignorant — there is nothing in the home. They will send the children to a Jewish day school because it is a good school or they are dissatisfied with the other schools in the community. People have taken the school and made the school the master of their child's destiny and it is stupid. Parents teach their children; the school only has them for a couple of hours a day.

Isolation

Many rabbis feel a sense of isolation in dealing with the issue of intermarriage. This isolation can take a number of forms. First, they may feel isolated from other rabbis. Other than infrequent regional or national conferences, the subject of intermarriage and how rabbis deal with the phenomenon is not often discussed. Most rabbis, both congregational and non-congregational, are caught up in the events of everyday life (as are most other professionals) and do not have much time to think, reflect or share their feelings about intermarriage or how they cope with the many problems that intermarriage presents to them both personally and professionally. The sense of isolation can be profound. Because rabbis have so many ambivalent feelings, they may also be reluctant to freely share or discuss the wide range of emotions they have about whether or not to perform intermarriages, how to cope within their own families when someone intermarries, and so on. Rabbis may also feel isolated from their congregants. If they are not ideologically compatible with most of their congregants or even a significant faction, then they may experience feelings of separateness over the issue. Those who are ideologically opposed to their denomination's official approach to intermarriage may also feel isolated from their own institutional structure. They may feel "left out there," unsupported by either their colleagues or the official structure of the denominational movement.

Feelings of isolation are often accompanied by feelings of being under siege. On a day-to-day basis, rabbis have to confront some issue concerning intermarriage. Some have to develop emotional walls not to feel hurt or betrayed, insulted or helpless. The siege mentality for some results in erecting and retreating behind some ideological wall that does not allow them to think about or feel their own reactions to deal with congregants, families, and the community as a whole concerning the issue. The sense of isolation can become self-fulfilling: feeling besieged leads to less openness, and a greater inability to effectively cope with their own reactions.

Anxiety and Powerlessness on the Home Front

If it is difficult to teach about intermarriage in a religious school full of children from intermarried families, difficult to protect members of one's synagogue youth group from marrying non-Jews, and difficult to instill a love of Judaism even in a day school — it is not so much easier at home. Rabbis — from all of the denominations — recognize that they have a limited amount of power even with regard to their own children's choices about whom to marry. The following three quotations, from a Reform, a Conservative and an Orthodox rabbi respectively, indicate that not even rabbis from the traditional movements think that their families are immune to what they all see as the threat of inter-marriage. Note the similarity among the remarks:

A Reform rabbi describes his lack of power (along with his optimism) in this regard:

> I think I would be foolish if I thought that our family's way of life would ensure that our children would marry spouses who were well suited for them in a religious sense. It is something that I worry about like any other parent, but I'm content in the knowledge that we have done our best to raise our kids in a way that they would want Judaism to be a part of their life, and they wouldn't be comfortable with someone who couldn't share their background.

A Conservative rabbi recognizes that it is quite possible his children will fall in love with non-Jews:

> Thank God they all have a lot of non-Jewish friends and it is wonderful, but we have made it clear how we feel. If they have a serious relationship with someone who is non-Jewish, I will probably take the tack of conversion. I feel very strongly that in this day and age we can not expect that all Jews are going to fall in love with Jews. Kids go off to college and they are going to meet non-Jews.

An Orthodox rabbi acknowledges that his children are subject to the vicissitudes of love and American culture:

> My children wouldn't say that they didn't know what they were doing. It would have to be some strong emotional attraction. Love is not a rational emotion. I would tell them that I wouldn't be at the wedding and I wouldn't participate. I wouldn't write them off. I think what a parent needs to do is to put up as strong a front before it happens as is humanly possible...After the fact, struggle with it...There are carry-over issues. There could be issues like will the grandchildren be Jewish or not. I think you have to struggle with that.

If a rabbi considers intermarriage to be a threat to the survival of the Jewish people — perhaps even on a par, in potential diminution of the people, with the Holocaust, and if a rabbi knows that his or her own children might very well marry non-Jews, there can be little wonder that that rabbi would feel anxious and powerless. But those feelings of anxiety and powerlessness are magnified by the sense that so few people understand or share those emotions. Indeed, rabbis often feel buffeted by demands to do what they cannot in good conscience do.

Frustration with Congregants' Demands

A common theme in our discussions with rabbis was their frustration with congregants' demands. We have seen how, in the presence of many intermarried couples, sermons about intermarriage need to navigate a fine line. It is not only in presenting sermons, however, that rabbis feel discomfort with the presence of intermarried couples in the synagogue. How should the non-Jews be integrated into synagogue life? Should they be granted full membership status, be allowed to serve on committees and participate in services? Because we will discuss in Chapter 3 the policies that rabbis and their synagogue boards have established with regard to the role of non-Jews in the synagogue, we will not visit the policy issues at this time. But for a taste of the kind of pressure and frustration felt by some rabbis in the face of these sorts of questions, we turn to a Reform rabbi:

> I took a stand several years ago that a non-Jew is limited in his or her participation in the religious life of the congregation. Number one, they cannot vote. By voting at a poorly attended meeting, twenty non-Jews could turn it into a church or make decisions about what we do or not do as a synagogue. As far as being officers of the congregation, it is not permitted in the synagogue too because there has to be a differentiation between a Jew and a non-Jew. I don't want the

congregation to have a non-Jewish president. I can't go into the Church and become the Pope either.

It is as if the Reform rabbi is saying, what do they expect of me? How far do they want me to go? Can't they understand that I am a rabbi and that this is a synagogue? He finds himself in the position of needing to lay down the law, of protecting a dividing line between Jews and non-Jews. But one can tell by his language — "I took a stand" — "I can't become the Pope, either" — that he faces considerable pressure to let non-Jews become full voting members of his synagogue. It is not easy to withstand such pressure.

We find more evidence of rabbis' frustration with congregants' demands in the explanations the rabbis use about why they do not officiate at intermarriages. Clearly feeling pushed by some congregants or community members to officiate, Rabbi Mark Joel Mahler (R) explains why he does not (1992):

...A recent study by demographer Egon Mayer for the American Jewish Committee reports that, in determining the Jewish fate of an intermarried couple, whether a rabbi officiates or not at an intermarriage has no appreciable effect whatsoever.

Why officiate, why violate the tradition, this argument runs, if officiating does not help the intermarried couple remain Jewish? Without putting words into Rabbi Mahler's mouth, it would not be far-fetched to assume that the subtext of his sermon has an even sharper edge: "Why are you urging me to do what I cannot do, and what would not be good for the Jews? Get off my back!" Rabbi Michael Zedek (R, 1992) draws upon the same study, using remarkably similar language as a partial explanation of his stand against officiation:

...the latest studies by *the* expert in the field, Dr. Egon Mayer, indicated that there is *no* evidence, *none*, that a rabbi's officiating brings the couple closer to the Jewish world. (emphasis in the original)

Again, we hear the message: "Dear Congregants Who Think I Should Officiate: My officiating wouldn't help intermarried couples stay Jewish. Stop asking!" The frustration is palpable.

If it is a bit odd for rabbis to argue that their decisions and potential actions do not have much of an impact on their congregants, it is no doubt a symptom of the general feeling of powerlessness rabbis feel against what they again and again call "the rising tide of intermarriage." There's just no way to fight it, and no way to win, whichever stand one takes. No wonder, then, that an overwhelming feeling on the part of the rabbis we studied is not a singular feeling at all, but a confusing mixture of feelings. In a word, rabbis feel ambivalent about all of the issues surrounding intermarriage. We turn now to examine that ambivalence.

AMBIVALENCE

Most rabbis have extreme feelings of ambivalence about the issue of intermarriage. Many are uncertain about how best to approach many aspects of the issue. Some take strong public stands and state what seem to be emphatic or even rigid views. But these external pronouncements do not reveal the internal uncertainty. Often there is a sense of confusion about which approach to take, which standards to uphold or not to uphold, or how to deal with each specific family. Ambivalence and confusion may evolve into different behaviors and feelings over time: As circumstances change, so may a rabbi's approach. A rabbi who believed that prevention was a "correct" strategy may change to the view that outreach is the best way to approach intermarriage, or vice versa.

Ambivalence also involves pain, sometimes expressed as feeling hurt for the families because they are hurting, or for the individuals who are struggling to cope with many of the problems that arise with intermarried couples. Intermarried couples themselves often experience hurt and pain in trying to resolve issues of religious identity, especially in terms of raising children. Families struggle about whether or not a child should be baptized, whether or not a child should receive a religious education, whether or not children should be allowed to date non-Jews, and so on. Rabbis find themselves in the middle of these painful family decisions and dilemmas and often absorb the feelings of the people around them.

Rabbis also feel their own pain. If they are in the position of refusing to marry a congregant whom they have known since childhood, or the relative of a close friend, or even their own children, it can be very painful and difficult for the rabbi to cope. Constantly facing difficult moral decisions is in itself painful for the rabbi. Uncertainty coupled with the anger that is sometimes directed against them can produce very painful responses on the part of rabbis, especially when they are isolated. Since they often believe that intermarriage is a serious threat to the structure of the Jewish community, they feel the sense of loss every time someone intermarries or raises their children out of the faith. It is one of the most painful realities of their profession, and produces a feeling of dismay.

Accepting and Rejecting — "Somehow We Change Our Face"

Whether a rabbi officiates at intermarriages or not, and no matter how certain he or she feels about his or her decision in that regard, almost every rabbi involved in this study strives, on some level, to embrace what might be called the core paradox of the rabbis' relationships with intermarriage: how to discourage intermarriage while simultaneously welcoming intermarried couples into active participation in synagogue life. A Reform rabbi sums up the paradox this way:

> What we are objecting to is the decision [to intermarry], not to the people involved. We say that we want you to be connected and we certainly realize that the Jewish spouse may still want to be connected and we are not rejecting him as a person or her as a person.

An extremely gentle reformulation of "hate the sin, not the sinner," this approach nonetheless runs the risk of alienating the intermarried couple. One can imagine a response on the part of such a couple — "you like me, you like my husband, it's our marriage you can't stand." The rabbis are relying on fine distinctions here.

Yet again and again, rabbis affirm their attempt to embrace this paradox. They also describe the odd, conflicted situation that embracing the "don't get intermarried/welcome the intermarried" paradox puts them in. Here is a typical sentiment, expressed by a Conservative rabbi:

> While we do everything possible to minimize the possibility of intermarriage, once it is a fact we should turn around and let them know that there is a place in our community for them — certainly for the Jewish spouse, and for the non-Jewish spouse that he or she could be present. Somehow we change our face and let people know that is how we feel.

The Conservative rabbi's painful but eloquent "somehow we change our face" is perhaps the best possible expression of the warring emotions that many rabbis feel with regard to intermarriage.

Even in Orthodox circles, there is hope that a Jew who has intermarried can somehow be "kept in," and that the non-Jewish spouse will choose to join the Jewish people. Here is an Orthodox rabbi, expressing an Orthodox version of the "disapprove, then accept" paradox, when asked what becomes of a member of his congregation who has intermarried:

> ...Nobody throws them out. I won't perform the wedding — that goes without saying. If a person chooses to marry out...we don't acknowledge the wedding, but we still receive the person with acceptance. You don't throw somebody out. Hopefully there will be a conversion.

Again we see the "changing of the face" — you are angry, disappointed, full of rejection, and you turn around and work to feel warm, accepting, hopeful.

In articulating the necessity for this kind of quick-change action, some rabbis acknowledge that such a move might appear self-contradictory. Rabbi Mark Kunis (O) writes:

> First of all, we've got to show our children and grandchildren how important Judaism is for us, how important that they marry Jews and have a Jewish family. Secondly — and you may think this is antithetical to the first, but it is not — we've got to change our attitude toward intermarried couples...

We can hear these same two almost-but-not-quite antithetical voices speaking, one after another, in Rabbi Donald Rossoff's (R) *Yom Kippur* sermon (1992):

> It [intermarriage] jeopardizes Jewish continuity, and...if one cares about having a Jewish family, having Jewish children and grandchildren, connecting with the past, present and future of the Jewish people, it is much more likely to happen, much easier to accomplish with another Jew — a Jew by birth or a Jew by choice — and more difficult with someone who does not a priori share the same values and goals.
>
> But 52% of Jews are choosing partners who are not Jewish. And so when a Jew chooses to intermarry and still be part of this adventure we call Jewish life, I think it important to affirm and support that choice to the extent that we honestly can. That is why I and this Temple are as open to inter-

married families as we are. I think that is best for your families and in the interest of Jewish continuity.

The two strains of thought, put more tersely, are these: intermarriage jeopardizes the future of the Jewish people, and intermarried Jews *are* the future of the Jewish people. It is a difficult contradiction; it is even more difficult to know what kind of policies to adopt that would support both lines of thinking. And that is why, as we have alluded to above, rabbis are deeply ambivalent about their policy decisions regarding officiation at intermarriage.

Ambivalence Regarding the Officiation Decision

Writing in the *Cleveland Jewish News*, Rabbi Daniel Roberts (R; 1993) names contradictory emotions he feels — heart and compassion on one hand, competing with "conscience and conviction" on the other:

> I watch the couple slowly walk away down the hall outside my office. I close the door and slouch down in my seat. I hurt. How I hate turning down the request of one of my former students to officiate at his wedding. His future mate is a lovely woman from a nice family. There is only one problem: She is not Jewish...
> ...I wish no engaged couple would have to leave a rabbi's office or hang up the telephone thinking that the rabbi is callous and unconcerned about their wedding request. Rabbis agonize and hurt, too! Sometimes I wish I could follow the dictates of my heart and ignore what I perceive as my dedication to God, Torah, and the people Israel. Sometimes it would make life easier, but conscience and conviction perched on each shoulder whisper, "No."

Rabbi James Rosenberg (R) puts the feeling of ambivalence even more starkly, describing it as a war within himself. He reveals his inner turmoil during a *Rosh Hashanah* sermon (1992):

There have been many occasions when my refusal to officiate at an interfaith marriage has led to a war between Rabbi Rosenberg and Jim Rosenberg. I remember well a conversation I had some years ago with a friend and colleague. It was a hot summer day, and he had come to visit me for the afternoon. We had just finished lunch and were walking down Water Street in Warren. We began to talk about the issue of rabbis officiating at interfaith marriages. Neither of us does. Paul turned to me and asked: "Do you ever feel that you may have made the wrong decision in your refusing to officiate?" To which I responded: "Almost every day."

Rabbis like Roberts and Rosenberg who do not officiate at intermarriages clearly have reason to feel ambivalent — they are in the position of saying "no" to people they care about. It may be surprising to find that some of those who do officiate feel a degree of pain and ambivalence about their decision, as well. While this group seems less likely to articulate their ambivalence publicly, a Reform rabbi privately expressed mixed feelings that are representative:

...There is no question that when I marry two committed Jews that I feel at my most sacred moment. There is no question in my mind that there is a difference for me between marrying two Jews and a Jew and a non-Jew. There is no question in my mind that the link is stronger when you marry two Jews together...It would be wonderful if Jews only married other Jews and if those were the only weddings that took place, but that is not the way that it is...

Put simply, the Reform rabbi would rather marry Jews to other Jews — marrying a Jew to a non-Jew is not quite as sacred an event; he would rather such marriages did not take place. Roberts does not perform intermarriages, and he is in pain about it; another Reform rabbi does, and he feels wistful about it. For rabbis who frequently encounter couples who wish to intermarry, there seems to be little hope of feeling whole-hearted about the situation.

RESPECTING RABBIS ON THE OTHER SIDE

While we have seen considerable anger between rabbis on either side of the officiation issue, members of those groups also have some softer words for one another. There are many, in fact, who voice quiet, if conflicted, respect for their colleagues on the other side of the fence — because the truth is, they have mixed feelings about the issue. The following passage demonstrates that a Conservative rabbi for example, is clearly aggrieved by the idea of a rabbi performing an intermarriage. He goes so far as to call intermarriages "anti-Jewish." On the other hand, he expresses relief at being able to refer his congregants to just such a rabbi:

> ...I think that the act of intermarriage is so anti-Jewish to the community and the Jewish home that for a rabbi to sanctify that marriage with Jewish liturgy evoking God's name, I can't do it. I am glad, however, that there are some people out there that do do it...Because I know that the work that they are doing is helping these people stay attached in some way. There is a rabbi here in town that I refer people to continually. We have a very good relationship even though there is an irony about it. In principle, I don't think that rabbis should do it, but yet I am glad that there is someone out there doing it.

A Reform rabbi does not himself officiate at intermarriages; nonetheless, he is able to accept the opposite decision on the part of his colleagues. He recognizes that there are legitimate reasons for taking the other side:

> ...I would credit any rabbi who was struggling with this issue as much as I have with integrity and real deep feeling and con-

cern about people with the right to do whatever he or she chooses to do, and feel what people do out of a matter of conscience and conviction is to be respected.

When asked her feelings on rabbis who officiate at intermarriage ceremonies, a Reform rabbi echoes these sentiments:

...I know that everyone's goal is ultimately to embrace Jews and help them find their path to involvement. So I don't have any interest in belittling those who make choices different than mine, any more than I would hope they would do the same. I'm grateful because I can refer people.

Standing firm in their decision not to officiate intermarriages, these rabbis nonetheless take solace in the fact that there are rabbis who do, and thus reveal their own ambivalence about the matter.

Coming from the other side, another Reform rabbi respects and even defends those who have decided *not* to officiate at intermarriages, though he himself does officiate. He tells congregants who complain to him about other rabbis that "any rabbi who truly wrestles with this does so out of a sincere love for the Jewish people."

For many rabbis, then, the officiation decision really could come down either way. The test of a rabbi's integrity seems to be whether or not he or she has really struggled with the question. It is a kind of puzzle, but a prevalent phenomenon, that rabbis who believe that both sides of the officiation decision are in some sense legitimate, nonetheless agonize over what their own personal policy should be. Perhaps it is precisely the high degree of ambivalence that leads to a great deal of angst. When one sees many shades of gray, making policy decisions is very difficult, as we shall explore more fully in the next chapter.

DISINTEREST IN THE INTERMARRIAGE "CRISIS"

In contrast to those who agonize over the question of officiation, and to those who see outreach toward intermarried couples as one of their primary concerns, many rabbis feel that the uproar in the national Jewish community about intermarriage represents a real misplacement of priorities and energy. Focus on the vibrancy of Jewish life, runs this argument, and concentrate less on the intermarriage phenomenon and on intermarried couples.

Here is a quick sampling of views from across the denominational spectrum. A Reform rabbi puts this argument most vehemently:

> Read Isaiah about the remnant of Israel...My position is to stop screaming and get over it. I really think that the Jewish issues need to be more on quality of what we do [and not on intermarriage]. I think that if we are educating to Judaism and to living Jewish lives the identity will take care of itself. I don't have time [to worry about intermarriage]. I am too busy teaching, and speaking, and living a Jewish life. I accept that many people are on their own way. My survival does not depend upon them. When they are ready, they will find their way back...I find it is reduction of Judaism that we are so desperately obsessed. I will say it again, if we worry less and live more with greater integrity as Jews — stop focusing so much on intermarriage; start nurturing Jewish living.

The Reform rabbi uses the word "obsessed" to describe the Jewish community's attention to intermarriage and "continuity." Rabbi Gerald Zelermyer (C) shares this view, similarly finding the Jewish community to be unreasonably preoccupied with intermarriage:

> I do agree that the Jewish community as a whole has too much of an obsession with intermarriage. The energy to pre-

vent it neither seems workable nor worth it. We need to connect with our essential mission as Jews. ...

A Conservative rabbi concurs, urging the Jewish community to focus on what is "strong and good":

I think there are a lot of resources that we are spending trying to deal with people who are intermarried and have really chosen not be a part of the Jewish community. We need to spend the money on people who have chosen to be part of the Jewish community. If we do something that is strong and good, if our program is creating a sense of worth, then that's the best advertising and marketing that we can do. You don't have to put ads in the newspaper...I do not deal with the issue of intermarriage. It is a negative issue, it is a negative agenda.

An Orthodox rabbi argues that resources should be directed to those who are most likely to stay Jewish — couples in which both partners are Jewish — rather than focusing on outreach to intermarried couples:

I think there is more need for inreach than outreach. Intermarriage can not be the only focus. We have to look at whether we are educating Jews about Judaism, or what are we doing to keep Jews Jewish. Right now I think that is a key issue. Where should the limited resources be going? Should they be going to work with intermarrieds or should more be going to working Jewish couples — those that are on the fringe, those that need more attention and a little more motivation to come in.

This wide range of feelings, often ambivalent, translates into an equally diverse set of actions, activities, approaches and behaviors. These behaviors are personally, institutionally and/or communally expressed.

CHAPTER 3

WHEN RABBIS TAKE ACTION

I n the previous chapter, we explored rabbis' feelings with regard to intermarriages. Of course, rabbis do more than feel pain or possibility, anxiety or assurance, in response to intermarriages — they also take action. They set guidelines regarding officiating at marriages; they refer or refuse to refer engaged couples to other rabbis; they encourage or deter conversion. They teach children and adults, facilitate outreach programs, guide synagogue policy, participate in committee meetings, write sermons and articles, counsel congregants, consult with fellow rabbis. They visit the sick, eulogize the dead, name the newborn. These activities often are affected by the presence of non-Jews in the synagogue community, and by rabbis' complicated and sometimes conflicting feelings about intermarriage. The task of this chapter is to explore what rabbis actually do, given the feelings we have already explored.

Whether or not they agree to officiate at intermarriages, all rabbis have a set of nuanced choices to make with regard to their interaction with couples who plan to intermarry. If a rabbi does *sometimes* officiate at intermarriages, but not just for anyone who asks, what conditions does he or she impose? If the rabbi never officiates at intermarriages, will he or she nonetheless counsel the couple? Bless them at services? Allow them to be members of the synagogue? Allow them to be married in the synagogue? Attend the wedding? What role will he or she allow an intermarried Jew to play in the synagogue? What about the non-Jewish partner?

Few rabbis have a blanket prohibition against involvement with couples contemplating intermarriage; even fewer give blanket acceptance to interfaith marriage ceremonies. The rabbis sort out each event, each act. For example, there are those rabbis who will not officiate at the wedding ceremony, nor bless the couple publicly, but who will work with the couple privately to create a wedding ceremony with Jewish elements. There are rabbis who will not co-officiate at a wedding ceremony with clergy from another religion, but who will welcome that clergy to give a blessing at the wedding reception. And there are many other variations on these themes. In this chapter, we examine these variations, analyzing the subtle distinctions the rabbis make between one intermarriage-related act and another.

Rabbis Who Do Not Officiate: Ostracism vs. Acceptance

A number of rabbis understand themselves to be "holding down the fort" against intermarriage. Their involvement in intermarriages consists of their doing whatever they can to express extreme disapproval at the phenomenon and to limit its occurrence. They preach about the disastrous effects intermarriage has on the Jewish people and on individual families. Such rabbis will not officiate at nor attend intermarriages; neither will they refer couples to rabbis who do officiate. One of the characteristics of this anti-intermarriage position is that it admits very little ambiguity. While the majority of rabbis swim in murky waters of mixed-messages, these rabbis send a clear signal.

The rabbis we studied represent primarily the Reform, Conservative, and Modern Orthodox movements. It will be instructive, however, to read part of an open letter sent to the Jewish Press by Agudath Israel of America, an association of very traditional Orthodox rabbis. Representatives of Agudath Israel wrote in alarmed response to what they saw as a muddying of the waters by the Rabbinical Council of America (RCA), a modern Orthodox group they would have expected to join them in their clear siren cry against intermarriage. The issue at hand was the acceptability of participation in synagogue life by the Jewish partner of an intermarriage. Rabbi Simcha J. Cohen of the "RCA Roundtable" had written a paper suggesting that it might be *halachically* acceptable for the Jewish partner of an intermarriage to be counted in a *minyan*. Afraid that this *halachic* argument creeps towards an acceptance of intermarriage, the Agudath Israel members admonished:

> Let there be absolutely no ambiguity: Intermarriage is not tolerable.
>
> Whether or not intermarriage in any given case is an act of conscious rejection or rebellion, it is always an act of destruction — one that strikes at the very essence of Jewish identity. In its own pernicious way, intermarriage jeopardizes Jewish survival no less than the brute force of evil employed throughout the generations by the greatest enemies of the Jewish people.
>
> The appropriate response to the rising tide of American Jewish intermarriage is not for the Orthodox rabbinate publicly to advocate a relaxation of Orthodoxy's "universally and consistently harsh" attitude toward intermarriage, as the RCA Roundtable proposes, but rather to seek ways to strengthen the sense of absolute taboo surrounding intermarriage.

There is, indeed, very little ambiguity about Agudath Israel's stand: couples who consider intermarriage should face an "absolute taboo." Rabbi Moshe Tendler, a well-known and highly respected Orthodox rabbi agrees with Agudath's conviction that counting intermarried Jews in a *minyan* implies acceptance of intermarriage. He urges his fellow rabbis not to give the impression of even the shadow of such acceptance:

...Intermarriage is a uniquely heinous sin. It is a total rejection of the historicity of Judaism, and the destiny of the Jewish Nation. If the mother be non-Jewish, the Jewish spouse knowingly, willingly, gives birth to children who belong to a "foreign nation." These children may well become our implacable foes, desirous of our destruction...Intermarriage is naked, undisguised, rebellion.

....Those who "marry out" throw down the gauntlet of rejection of our faith community. The traditional *Halachic* decision is to respond to this rejection by rejection. It is as valid today as it was centuries ago. Modification of this response, moderation of our abhorrence, would denigrate the dignity of *Hashem* and his chosen people. Such insult cannot be ignored. Moral turpitude must not be rewarded by social acceptance as it is today. When our *rabbonim* permit those who married non-Jewish spouses to...[be] given honors during services; or allowed to hold elected office in the *shul* administration, we remove the only barrier to intermarriage — other than Torah education — social sanction!

Steps Toward Acceptance

While it is certainly true that the "social sanction" advocated here by Tendler is a time-honored response to intermarriage, this sort of stand might be more rhetorical than practical, even in Orthodox circles. The Modern Orthodox rabbis we interviewed do not in practice enact strong sanctions in the face of intermarried congregants. An Orthodox rabbi explains what he does when approached by an intermarried Jew interested in joining his congregation:

When someone comes to me and says, "I don't know if I am eligible to join because I am intermarried," it's my responsibility to say, "Yes, you are eligible to join. There are other people who have done it already...being intermarried does not make you not Jewish anymore." A Jew who wants to do any of the *mitzvot* or practices that are part of Judaism, I say, should be encouraged to do that, and should be helped, insofar as it is possible.

Describing his Orthodox congregation as "welcoming and accepting," the Orthodox rabbi explains just how unworkable a policy of ostracism would be in his community:

> Only if the intermarriage rates were 15% or 1.5% the strategy which says that intermarriage is such an assault against our community that we will ostracize anyone who does it — that strategy would have a lot more in its favor. *We* could ostracize *them*. But I don't see how that's a viable strategy when *we* are small and they are many. We can't ostracize them. That's backwards. (emphasis in original)

Another Orthodox rabbi outlines the slightly colder reception intermarried people would find in his synagogue:

> [An intermarried] couple wouldn't feel comfortable at this congregation. Sometimes you will have the Jewish male...show up at the congregation from time to time...He might show up and usually if he shows up it is for a reason like his mother or father dies. He is not going to feel comfortable. We have a small congregation and people know each other. Let's say that he is from out of town and little by little it gets out that he is married to a non-Jew and then there is a pulling away and he will feel uncomfortable if nothing else because of his guilt. Eventually he will go somewhere else where he doesn't feel that guilt.

The rabbi avoids words or actions so stark as, "We reject him," and adopts, rather, the passive voice — "there is a pulling away" on the part of the congregation. "Pulling away," while certainly a message of disapproval, is a far cry from the "absolute taboo" or the "abhorrence" advocated in the letter from Agudath Israel. It is not easy to express abhorrence towards someone who comes into the synagogue to say *kaddish* no matter how angry or sad one feels about intermarriage. And so we have left the land of absolutes articulated and advocated in the letters by Agudath

Israel and by Moshe Tendler. We enter, instead, the murky, para-
doxical realm that characterizes most American rabbis' responses
to intermarriage — a realm where disapproval is tempered by
hospitality and acceptance is tainted with anxiety.

Take, for example, the actions of a Conservative rabbi. He disapproves of intermarriages in no uncertain terms. He will not
attend intermarriage ceremonies, whether performed by a rabbi
or a Justice of the Peace, and he will not refer congregants to rabbis who do officiate at intermarriages. Even the pull of the wedding of a family member has not been enough for him to break
his ban against attending intermarriages:

> I have had some members of my family intermarry, and I
> wouldn't even go...I think even going lends an air of legitima-
> cy to it.

He disapproves of rabbis who do "lend legitimacy" to intermarriages by performing them, and he tells his congregants that
he would "rather see them married by a Justice of the Peace" than
to imply that there is something Jewish about an intermarriage.

By refusing to attend intermarriage ceremonies or to refer
congregants to rabbis who perform them, this Conservative rabbi
tries to send as clear a message as possible of disapproval. And yet
even he finds it impossible and undesirable to participate in the
sort of negative social sanction Tendler advocates. Far from it.
Intermarried non-Jews are allowed to be members of his synagogue, restricted only from performing "ritual honors," such as
blessing the Torah.[6] This Conservative rabbi notes, apparently
with some pride, about non-Jewish members of the synagogue
that "with the exception of the ritual honors...they are very much
part of the synagogue life and they are equal in every respect." It

---

[6] The Conservative movement has guidelines noting that non-Jews should not
be allowed to be members of the congregation. This Conservative synagogue
would not be in adherence with this guideline.

goes without saying that *Jewish* partners in intermarried couples are allowed full participation in the life of his synagogue. Even when refusing to officiate at an intermarriage, he does what he can to communicate affection, concern, and acceptance of the couple:

> ...What I say to them is that I cannot be there for you at your wedding, but please understand that I will be thinking of you. I hope you will understand why I can't do it, and I hope even more so you will recognize that my saying no to that is not my slamming the door shut. It is saying that we still want to see you and you are still a part of this congregation. I point to all the families who are very happy members of the Temple who are intermarried.

Many rabbis share this Conservative rabbi's strategy of trying to remain connected to the couple through counseling and by inviting them to join the synagogue. Some of those who, like this rabbi, refuse to officiate at intermarriages, nonetheless do refer couples to other rabbis; some who will not themselves officiate are willing to attend intermarriage ceremonies.

Like this rabbi, another Conservative rabbi refuses to attend mixed-marriage ceremonies, even when family members are involved. In a letter which he hopes will help preempt such an eventuality, he tells his nieces and nephews:

> ...If at some point you do decide to intermarry, I want you to know where I stand. As a rabbi, even though it will be very painful, I and my family would not be able to attend the wedding.

The Conservative rabbi warns, in other words, that he is willing to enact a strong negative social sanction. It is even more extreme in its being enacted against, as he writes, "nieces and nephews about whom I especially care." And yet he immediately follows up this warning with an incredible softening:

...However, this does not in any way mean that we would want to cut off our relationship. I would be there for you in the future, to counsel you if you needed, to support you and your future family in any way that I could.

This Conservative rabbi would not be willing to be at the wedding, but he would "be there" in the future for support and guidance. As we noted in Chapter 2, he also softens his stand by being willing to refer congregants to rabbis who do officiate at mixed-marriages. Recall his thinking:

I think that the act of intermarriage is so anti-Jewish to the community and the Jewish home that for a rabbi to sanctify that marriage with Jewish liturgy evoking God's name, I can't do it. I am glad, however, that there are some people out there that do do it.

Simultaneous Messages of Disapproval and Support

Many other rabbis seek — through word and deed — to send a simultaneous message of disapproval and support. Consider the words of Rabbi Jack Moline (C), taking great pains to make the two parts of the message clear:

L'chat'chila, this is, before the fact, I am an opponent of inter-marriage. I do not believe that two people of different religions should marry. If they love each other so much, one of them should convert or both of them should find a third tradition. B'diavad, after the fact, I am in favor of marriage. Once a couple has formed a family, everything possible should be done to make certain the relationship is sustained.
Let me make it even clearer. Right up to the moment when the officiant says, "you are now husband and wife," I hold out the hope that one or the other will say, "just a minute, something is not right here." Once the man has left his mother and the woman left her home and traveled on to where the two shall be as one, the business at hand is creating a stable and loving family. Period.

Rabbi Moline uses a principle of Talmudic logic used by many other rabbis to justify what might otherwise seem like an odd change of face: *l'chat'chila* one must disapprove; *b'diavad* one must support. The transformation in attitude is to occur at the instant the judge or clergy pronounces the couple married.

One might wonder how it is possible to transform one's feelings and actions on a dime. How do rabbis do it? How does this combination of "disapproval and support" express itself in the deeds of rabbis who do not officiate at intermarriages? As we have seen, support is expressed as the rabbi counsels the couple, refers them to another rabbi, welcomes them to join the synagogue. Some rabbis draw the line, though, at any action which can be perceived to be a ritual endorsement of the intermarriage. Rabbi Stuart M. Geller (R), writing in his synagogue bulletin, marks this boundary:

> ...Though it is understood that I do not perform interfaith marriages, it is apparently not clear why it would be inappropriate for me to do wedding blessings for couples where one partner is not Jewish...
>
> ...It is my goal, and my obligation as a Rabbi, to nurture Judaism, to teach about our religion, and to pass it on to the next generation. I think that part of that teaching, and part of that instruction, includes passing on a clear and understandable message...
>
> ...The wedding blessing is theologically linked to the wedding. It also takes place on the Pulpit on *Erev Shabbat* and by the Rabbi. This is Jewish...When we invite an interfaith couple on to the Pulpit for a blessing, are we not giving a mixed -message? It is not clear to the Congregation why such a couple can stand on the Pulpit on Friday night and celebrate with the Congregation, but cannot come on to the same Pulpit on Sunday morning and be married by the same Rabbi.

Rabbi Geller's desires, in his words, to send "a clear and understandable message," to avoid sending a "mixed-message." He worries that if he blesses an intermarrying couple at services, his congregants will wonder why he should not be able to marry them as well. And so Rabbi Geller refuses to perform the blessing along with refusing to perform the wedding — in the name of consistency. But, as seems to be inevitable, and like some other rabbis, Rabbi Geller does send a mixed-message. For in the very same column, indeed in the very same paragraph in which he explains why he cannot bless the couple from the pulpit, he also says, "Of course, I, and we all, wish the couple well. We each give them our blessing in our own ways." And he goes on to say:

> ...Our Congregation is sensitive to the many lives that are touched when a couple intermarries. In response, our Synagogue offers a variety of programs such as Introduction to Judaism classes, groups for parents of interfaith couples, interfaith discussion groups for the couples, workshops for teenagers and religious school teachers, etc.
>
> These particular programs, and the atmosphere of the Temple itself, allow everyone a framework to discuss, explore, and reach an understanding of the many complicated issues involved. Perhaps, more importantly, the Rabbi has always encouraged personal contact and discussions with the couples and their parents. The Rabbi will work with the couples and their families to plan appropriate and meaningful ceremonies. This is his blessing.

The column written expressly to clarify why the rabbi cannot bless an intermarried couple at services thus ends proclaiming the many ways in which the rabbi and the congregation as a whole do indeed bless the couple, or at least meet some of their emotional needs. On the one hand, Rabbi Geller is making a coherent distinction between the kind of blessing that he might give during a public religious ceremony and the kind of counseling that he can give privately. Of course, blessings and counseling are different, although some may view counseling as a de facto blessing. On the other hand, one might view the whole thing as an elaborate defense of hair-splitting, a valiant effort to claim consistency while acting and feeling ambivalent. On yet a final hand, one might argue that unless one is prepared to take the unbending stand of Agudath Israel or Rabbi Tendler, responding to "rejection with rejection," one is left with little choice but to attempt to deal with multiple levels of ambivalence.

Referrals to Other Rabbis

One Reform rabbi tries to hold a consistent line. Unwilling to officiate at intermarriages, neither will he attend them. Indeed, as we saw, this same Reform rabbi in Chapter 2 went so far as to cut off communications with a daughter while she dated a non-Jew. And yet, when it comes to referring congregants to rabbis who will perform intermarriages, he has modified his position:

> ...Years ago I didn't [refer to rabbis who officiate at mixed-marriages]. I was playing a game I guess. I didn't want to be involved... I don't do that anymore. I don't play games anymore. The word is out, so I would rather steer them to a rabbi who is sane — someone that might get them into some sort of program, who is in a congregational setting, and not just those who will take the money and disappear. I do refer now to rabbis who I think will at least speak to them about Judaism or have them promise to raise their kids Jewishly.

In a world where "the word is out," where everyone knows that there are rabbis who officiate at intermarriages, refusing to refer couples to such a rabbi seems to him like "playing a game," like avoiding reality. And so it is that this Reform rabbi chooses where to draw his line in the sand — officiating, no; attending, no; referring, yes.

One Conservative rabbi's appreciation of consistency forces him to disagree. To him, referring couples to rabbis who officiate at intermarriages is as out of line as officiating at the marriage itself. He unhappily finds himself increasingly isolated among Conservative colleagues:

> ...I have noticed with some horror that many of my Conservative colleagues have really softened their positions. When they raised their hands [at a conference] about who refers [couples to other rabbis] for intermarriage — half of my Conservative colleagues raised their hands. A Conservative rabbi has absolutely no business referring any more than performing an intermarriage. ...

And yet even this Conservative rabbi finds it necessary to accommodate the reality of high rates of intermarriage in various ways. When asked about the presence of intermarried couples in his synagogue, he says:

> First of all, they are all welcome. I think that we have all pretty much given up ostracism. That was a technique of the last generation...I don't do it nor have I ever done it. I don't believe in it. Someone who was married to a non-Jew I wouldn't be comfortable with as President of my *shul*. There are limits...If the non-Jewish partner is actively considering conversion, I will give them a lot of time. Even if they are not, I will make them welcome. However, they cannot be a member of my congregation, they cannot participate in the service. They can come to the service, and they are more than welcome. When they come, I will do my best to make them feel welcome. We try to be as clear about the limits of their participation as we can.

Read this rabbi's words again. The sentences alternate like the refrain of a sad song, "they are welcome/there are limits/they are welcome/there are limits..." Negative sanction and support, limits and welcomes. Again and again, rabbis find themselves playing with the percentages. What's better? 90% sanction, 10% support? 50/50? 1% sanction, 99% support? Support now, sanction later? The correct balance seems impossible to find for most rabbis.

Participation Without Officiation

Some rabbis come as close as they possibly can to officiating at an intermarriage ceremony, short of actually doing it. A Reform rabbi will not himself officiate at an intermarriage, and he strongly rejects the idea of a ceremony that integrates Jewish and Christian symbols:

> ...I...buy into the symbol systems. To bring them together — is a glass of wine the symbol of the joy of *Shabbat* or the symbol of the blood of the sacrifice of Jesus? I can understand why both partners would want to have themselves represented in that ceremony, but I don't feel at all comfortable with that, nor do I think that any rabbi should feel comfortable doing that. I support rabbis who do interfaith marriages, but I can't support those who do co-officiating.

And yet this Reform rabbi will attend mixed-marriages, and has offered a blessing to a mixed couple after the ceremony was over — "I certainly would be willing to do that even if they got married in a church somewhere."

While drawing the line at officiating, rabbis like this Reform rabbi clearly want to have some sort of impact on the couple. He urges couples who call him about officiating to come in to talk with him:

> ...I tell them that I want to be up front with them so that there is no misunderstanding. I say — "I don't feel comfortable performing an intermarriage. I know a number of rabbis in the field who do intermarriages for all the right reasons and who do a wonderful job and who I think you would really like to work with. But I am hesitant to give you a referral over the phone until I meet you." More often than not, people are willing to come in and talk. That for me has been important because it allows me to explain my position and allows me the opportunity to explore with them some of the issues of an interfaith marriage.

This Reform rabbi — like almost all of the rabbis we studied, immediately qualifies his negative sanctioning action — the refusal to officiate, with a supportive action, the invitation to come and talk. The proposed talk in the rabbi's office will provide a chance for support: he will provide the couple with a referral to a rabbi who "does a wonderful job." But the office meeting will also include a message of disapproval of sorts. He will take the chance to "explore the issues of an interfaith marriage" — that is, to alert the couple to the potential pitfalls of the decision they are making. Perhaps above all, the meeting will give him a chance to explain "his position," to explain why and how he can be at once so friendly and helpful and also be what people might see as so closed and rejecting. One sees why it would be a complicated message to try to send on the telephone.

This Reform rabbi does not walk on this particular tightrope alone. In just one of many such examples, Rabbi Mark Joel Mahler (R) draws very similar distinctions for his congregation in a sermon:

> ...I am always eager to meet with couples who are planning an intermarriage. For Egon Mayer's research...indicates that the option for the non-Jew to convert to Judaism is rarely mentioned by the Jewish partner or by the Jewish partner's family. I, therefore, want that opportunity. I want to say, "Have you ever considered converting to Judaism?" I want the opportunity to say that the divorce rate for Jews in intermarriages is about twice the divorce rate of Jews married to Jews. I want the opportunity to say that marriage is difficult under the best of circumstances, and the incontrovertible statistics indicate that intermarriage is not the best of circumstances. Surely, I want the opportunity to elaborate upon the many other reasons why I do not officiate at intermarriages.

Below, we will see other rabbis who, like Mahler, make a point of advocating conversion whenever possible. For now, it is worth noting just how important it is to him to have an opportunity both to warn the couple that they might be making a mistake, and also to get their understanding, if not forgiveness, for what Mahler fears will seem a very non-supportive, non-compassionate stand. Mahler wants the opportunity both to warn and to be warm.

A Conservative rabbi has given up trying to do what the Reform rabbi previously mentioned and Mahler want so fervently to do. She does not invite couples in to see her so that she can explain to them why she cannot officiate at their wedding. She has come to think that the need to explain represents the rabbi's need, not a need of the couple. Here is how she explains this decision:

> I no longer tell people why I don't do intermarriages and if they ask I just say I'm a member of the RA [Conservative Movement's Rabbinical Assembly] and I'm not allowed to. I have found that they are not really interested in my moaning and groaning about it.

She also feels no need to alert the couples, as the Reform rabbi and Mahler do, to the possible pitfalls of their upcoming marriage — unless the couple themselves seem to sense some of those pitfalls. Endeavoring to tell a couple that is not in pain why they should be in pain about their upcoming marriage will only serve to annoy the couple, the Conservative rabbi argues:

> If a couple calls and says, "We're intermarrying and we want to meet with a rabbi," then I tell them I don't do intermarriages. If they still want to meet, I assume that they are in some pain about this issue and that they are worth talking to. If people are not in any pain about it, you're not going to succeed in paining them, only annoying them.

Rather than alerting the couple to possible troubles ahead for them in their marriage, the Conservative rabbi does what she can to alert them to the troubles they might face planning their wedding. She lets them know the context in which they are intermarrying — it is a context in which intermarriage is an extremely heated issue, and the couple might unwittingly be a target for some of the heat. Here is what the Conservative rabbi reports saying to intermarried couples who call her asking her to officiate:

> I don't perform intermarriages. The reality is you may experience a run-around trying to find someone who does. Unfortunately, the Jewish community is obsessed about its own survival and has latched on to intermarriage as the issue which determines its fate. So, all those fears get pinned on any couple that decides to intermarry. It isn't fair. I hope that you will be able to see your way through it and find a place within the Jewish community anyway, even if you are not treated with the welcome you deserve.

And so, though she herself cannot officiate nor offer the welcome she would perhaps prefer to the intermarried couple, the Conservative rabbi seeks to send a message of warmth. Most important, of course, is her analysis of the situation — the Jewish community, in great pain about assimilation generally, regularly puts the onus of all of that pain on the shoulders of each individual intermarried couple just before their wedding. And in her words, it is not fair.

Rabbi Michael Zedek (R), too, wants to find a way to deliver a welcoming message to intermarried couples. He has found a way to hang onto his refusal to officiate at an intermarriage while taking a very active role in the preparation and enactment of the ceremony. In his *Yom Kippur* sermon in 1992, he explains with great excitement to his congregation that legally, one does not need "a judge, a priest, or a rabbi" to officiate at a wedding, rather, "all that is necessary is a valid, registered license." Here is how this realization helps Rabbi Zedek with the dilemma of participating without officiating, supporting while sanctioning:

...So I encourage couples and work with them to write their own ceremony, where they celebrate, sometimes officiate, and always affirm what's true about them, what they have found and hope to have even more as part of their lives together.

...I go to such weddings. I have participated, spoken at such celebrations, and I've offered a prenuptial [sic] blessing at a *Shabbat* service. *I will participate but I do not officiate.* So I call these the most beautiful weddings I've ever done, and they are an exceptional, integrity-filled and fully legal celebration of a growing — so we pray — a growing love. (rabbi's emphasis)

Helping plan, offering a blessing beforehand, speaking during the ceremony itself — Zedek gets as close to the line as one can while keeping his balance on the tiny bit of ground from which he can proclaim, "*I will participate but I do not officiate.*" And so he barely keeps himself among the ranks of the non-officiators.

Squeezed so close to the precipice, many other rabbis have decided to take the leap. They let go of the narrow distinction between "participation" and "officiation" and choose to officiate. But even for them, even for rabbis who do officiate at intermarriages, a dizzying terrain of choices about where and when and for whom to officiate remains. It is to their similar landscape of shifting shades of sanction and support that we now turn.

Rabbis Who Do Officiate: Setting the Conditions

Working Only with Those Who Plan to Convert

A Reform rabbi takes perhaps the most extreme stand among those who do officiate at intermarriages, performing ceremonies only for those intermarried couples whose non-Jewish partner has agreed to convert, sometime after the wedding. Acknowledging that she has been "burned" once, she nonetheless argues that her approach makes more sense than requiring someone to convert quickly in deference to a wedding date:

> ...I don't officiate, unless they are on a clear path to conversion — a clear path. It's not just study. It's that they're working with you; they're on their way. I won't it hold over someone's head, "You'd better convert by the wedding date or else." Because it doesn't work. It has people rushing and scurrying and panicked. But there has to be that pathway. We agree that we will conclude [the conversion], following the marriage.

The Reform rabbi sees her demand that the non-Jew be "on a clear path" to conversion as much more stringent than what some of her colleagues require of an intermarried couple before they will officiate — the commitment to raise any children of the marriage as Jews. She objects to this practice on the grounds that 1) at the time of a wedding, long before any children are born, it is very hard for a couple to agree to specifics of child-rearing, and 2) if the non-Jewish parent has not agreed to convert for him or herself, it is hard to imagine that there will be enough commitment and knowledge to raise Jewish children. The Reform rabbi explains:

> ...I think exacting a promise from them that they will raise a Jewish family is the most meaningless promise we can ask for. I think it belittles the couple and it belittles the process of raising Jewish children...I think there has to be some greater level of commitment. I have not yet found the way to get that outside of conversion.

Another Reform rabbi joins her criticism of those rabbis who agree to officiate at an intermarriage based on a promise that any children will be raised as Jews:

I do not ask questions about children, like will you raise the children Jewish...I think that plays into our Jewish survivalist *mishagas* — I don't matter, but *l'ma'an hayeladim*, for the sake of the children — the idea that the future counts but we do not. Clearly if children are a consideration then I am interested in the question, but I don't put that up front — I don't say, "It is okay for you to intermarry as long as your children are raised as Jews." It invalidates the adult in Jewish life.

Working Only with Synagogue Members

Focusing on the present life of the adult couple rather than on their potential children, the Reform rabbi, mentioned above, will officiate only at marriages (intermarried or otherwise) of synagogue members. If non-members call, he simply says that he cannot officiate. "I don't say to them on the phone, 'By the way if you join the synagogue, I'll think about it.' It's the other way around." He wants to have an on-going relationship with the couples for whom he officiates, so he limits his officiation to couples who are synagogue members, people who have indicated "involvement and continuity and commitment" through their affiliation with the community and the congregation.

Planning for the Children

Most of the rabbis we studied who officiate at intermarriages disagree with the two Reform rabbis previously mentioned. While they might require synagogue membership and some amount of study, most of them focus their requirements on the upbringing of potential children. We saw an example of this approach in Chapter 2, in Rabbi Raphael Asher's invitation to the non-Jewish partner to become a "coguardian of a Jewish Home." Rabbi Henry Cohen (R), in a letter to us, explains his similar approach quite simply:

...I am among those rabbis who officiate at mixed-marriages
if I am convinced that there is a sincere commitment to raise
the children as Jews in the sense of giving them a structured
Jewish education and if I believe the non-Jewish partner will
study Judaism.

Rabbi Bruce Kahn (R) spells out his requirements in more
detail:

...I will consent to do the marriage providing they are willing
to sit with me and:

1. We examine together the couple's religious views in the
areas of theology, life after death, prayer, ethics and ritual. We
examine their views and habits and resolve clashes among
them.

2. The couple vows to join a synagogue, to raise their children
as Jews and to establish a Jewish atmosphere in the home.
They must agree to keep these vows before them throughout
their marriage, lest they forget and pay drastic consequences
later.

3. They will study critically the history and content of Jewish
wedding ceremonies from ancient times to the present day.

4. They will create with me the most meaningful service possible, a wedding service no part of which excludes either partner, a service wherein every word and ritual must affirm both
the bride and the groom.

5. I promise the couple that at any time in the future they may
require my help to solve a problem or celebrate a blessing
regarding their marriage or family life I shall be available to
them...forever!

It is not clear what are the "drastic consequences" to which
Rabbi Kahn refers in stipulation number 2. But the point of the

list of commitments seems clear, and it has apparently indeed served as a filter of sorts — Rabbi Kahn proclaims in this same sermon that he has turned down intermarried couples and Jewish couples who have been unwilling to meet these conditions.

Officiating without Conditions

There is a group of rabbis who will perform intermarriages without exacting specific promises about Jewish practice. Some draw the line at co-officiating with non-Jewish clergy, but they do not require the couple to make vows about their present or future Jewish involvements. Indeed, Rabbi Marc Brownstein (R) argues explicitly against the idea of setting conditions on the couples whom he marries. Claiming that this is a sort of coercion which can only have a negative effect, he believes in "embracing" the couple, whatever their current level of Jewish commitment, and focusing on educating the children:

> ...The rate of interfaith marriage will remain the same and probably increase. Sanctions and coercion will not stop these marriages. The synagogue and rabbis must embrace the inter-married *with no limitations* and work diligently to instill Jewish commitments in their children. (emphasis added)

Rabbi Howard A. Berman (R) takes a similar stance against specific "limitations." In lieu of exacting promises, and placing great faith in his powers of persuasion, Rabbi Berman relies on an eye-to-eye, emotional exhortation:

> At the end of my first meeting with every couple at whose wedding I officiate, whether two Jews or interfaith, I look them straight in the eye...and confront them with the inescapable responsibility that rests upon their shoulders — whether they like it or not, whether they acknowledge it or not...that the decisions that each and every young Jew in the

world today make — about how they live their lives and raise their families — *will either be a seed for the future, or a nail in the coffin of the Jewish people...*

I remind every one of them that they are a direct, living link in a 5,000-year-old chain of faith and courage — of suffering and hope — that stretches back through time and space to Mt. Sinai...to Abraham...and they have to realize *that it could all end with them...*It's a pretty heavy trip to lay on a dewy-eyed, idealistic young couple, whose immediate concerns are perhaps not so cosmic. But it has been my experience that it touches their hearts and souls — both the Jew and the non-Jewish partner — and lets them know that the love and support we want to offer them is motivated *both* by a genuine, sincere personal interest — and ultimately, a transcendent mission.... . (All emphases and ellipses are Berman's — no text has been extracted from the original.)

Rabbi Berman finds that he touches "the hearts and souls" of the young people whom he marries with his admittedly conditional "love and support." It is love and support that has "a transcendent mission," love and support that is offered in the context of a stark warning, that the young couple not drive the "nail in the coffin of the Jewish people." It is another version of what is becoming a familiar formula — support served up with a dollop of guilt, love offered with a dose of fear.

Other rabbis back far away from what Berman himself calls this "heavy trip." Instead of focusing on how the couple will "raise their families" or how they will sort out potential conflicts in religious belief, a Reform rabbi focuses on the other factors in the couple's relationship:

...One of the principles upon which I operate is that if a relationship is healthy then the religion of the members of that relationship is a secondary issue. If the marriage is healthy, they will figure out a way to make the religious stuff work. If it is not healthy, that will be a factor in its demise...My primary rule about doing marriages is that if I don't think the relationship is a healthy one I refuse to do the wedding. Nothing else is as primary as that; everything else is secondary.

Though "everything else is secondary" to the health of the relationship for the Reform rabbi, he does place some limits on the sorts of ceremonies he will perform. He does not do ceremonies "in any building where there are Christian symbols present" he will not "co-officiate at a ceremony when Christian references are made," and he will not officiate on Saturday before sundown or on Jewish holidays.

Officiating with Christian Clergy and Christian Symbols

There are, finally, rabbis who will follow the wishes of the couple with regard to co-officiation and symbols of other religions. The Reform rabbi, whose description of a *bris* appears in Chapter 2, finds beauty in the strengths that intermarried couples bring to one another. He describes the movement in his thought and practice:

Although when I started to do intermarriages I insisted that the children be raised as Jewish, that there be a strong commitment to a Jewish home. I really put these people through the grill. Over time my position became increasingly liberalized. ...

Now the Reform rabbi feels comfortable co-officiating with non-Jewish clergy, and integrating the symbols of the non-Jewish partner into the ceremony. He explains:

The wave of the future is going to be what is absolutely necessary for human survival, and that is recognizing more and more the common ground that we share...I think it [intermarriage] is going to lead to a broadening of our vision. This is the only way that we are going to survive on this planet...There are not too many bigger things around than recognizing our common humanity...I don't see anything wrong with two people who love each other who want to get married and love each other's traditions. These are not bad things — these are good things. That kind of thing if allowed to continue can only lead to a better and better world.

Intermarriage, according to the Reform rabbi is not a "bad thing." On the contrary, it may lead the way to a better age. Rabbi Samuel Silver, quoted here from his book, *Mixed Marriage: Between Jew and Christian*, shares this notion:

> Idealists of all faiths have envisioned a time when all cultural groups will merge. The prophets of old anticipated an era when all men would recognize the value and validity of acknowledging the Deity and together they would "go up to the mountain of the Lord."
>
> ...Perhaps the intermarrying couples, motivated initially by romance, will become the harbingers of a new kind of world unity, in which not only couples but ideologies and theologies will live "happily ever after." (p. 94)

Thus with the Reform rabbi mentioned above and Silver, we have come full circle. We began with the rabbis of Agudath Israel and Rabbi Moshe Tendler who contest unequivocally that intermarriage is a pernicious, intolerable, heinous sin which must be greeted with the strongest social sanctions possible. We reviewed, then, the positions of a wide range of rabbis who, in one way or another, do equivocate. Clinging both to a desire to reject intermarriage and also to a belief that it is wrong to reject Jews, they balance hospitality with limitations, negative sanctions with support. And while probably neither side would warm to the comparison, we have returned, with a Reform rabbi, to a stance equal in its certitude to that of Agudath Israel. While the rabbis of Agudath Israel admonish that intermarriage is "always an act of destruction," the Reform rabbi exhorts that intermarriage "can only lead to a better and better world."

It is no wonder, given the competing, contradictory absolutes of the Reform rabbi and Agudath Israel, that most rabbis ride the fence in one way or another. But as we have seen, sending ambiguous messages has perils of its own. Rabbis want so much to provide leadership for their communities by standing for something clear. Happily, there is one goal around which most rabbis can rally with little hesitation, one place in the wide realm of intermarriage in which the rabbi can play a prominent and productive role — promoting conversion of the non-Jewish partner of an intermarried couple. We turn now to examine the rabbis' actions in that area.

THE CONVERSION SOLUTION

Judaism as an Answer to Some Non-Jews' Needs

As indicated in Chapter 2, many rabbis view conversion as a way out of what they consider the painful reality of intermarriage. Indeed, Rabbi Mark Kunis (O) welcomes the conversion of non-Jewish spouses, calling such conversions "an opportunity to celebrate and strengthen Jewish life." In this chapter, we note that some Reform rabbis require that the non-Jewish partner be on a path toward conversion before they will officiate at the wedding; and one Orthodox rabbi accepts the intermarried Jew into his congregation, saying "hopefully there will be a conversion." And so many rabbis, across denominational lines, actively encourage conversion of the non-Jewish partner, before or after the marriage ceremony.

In a *Yom Kippur* (1992) sermon, Rabbi Michael Zedek (R) joins many of his colleagues in admonishing his congregants to ask potential non-Jewish spouses or in-laws to convert:

...I have known many instances where a non-Jewish partner seriously would have considered conversion if only someone had asked, given some encouragement, if only the lover, spouse, an in-law had asked. If it matters, at least ask. Say so. After all, this 4,000 years long adventure of the Jewish people is a distinct, remarkable, and amazing journey, and you would, perhaps, be amazed how often the refrain: "This is what I've always believed. I just didn't know there was a group that did so. " It can be a wonderful gift.

Rabbi Andrew Warmflash (R) repeats the theme:

One thing we can do is to change our attitudes toward conversion. There is absolutely nothing wrong with encouraging someone you love to convert to Judaism as a prerequisite for marriage.

I often counsel people who are considering interfaith marriages and when I suggest this to them, they usually say something like: How can I ask him to give up his faith, when I am not willing to give up mine? For me, the answer is simple: First of all, there is nothing wrong with making demands on the people you love, it's done all the time. Secondly, since when is it such a sacrifice to become a Jew?

I really believe that when you encourage someone to convert to Judaism, you are giving them something far more valuable than what you are asking them to leave behind.

One Orthodox rabbi would be hesitant to actively encourage the non-Jewish member of a mixed couple to convert. Indeed, he says, converting because one is about to get married "is not the ideal reason for conversion to Judaism." On the other hand, the Orthodox rabbi makes the interesting point that a non-Jew might be drawn to a Jew precisely because he or she is genuinely drawn to Judaism. He finds that:

...a lot of times, the non-Jewish fiancé, spouse, or girlfriend of the Jew has actually looked for a Jew because that gives him or her a cover for going to talk to the rabbi — sometimes to the extent of going through the conversion even *after* the relationship breaks up. The relationship really served as cover for them to do that. Lots of times there is a long history to why a non-Jewish person would end up with a Jew...It is not simply "maybe I better think of conversion because his mother will never accept our marriage if I don't" which is something I really don't want to hear. I wouldn't be that interested in working with someone who wants to convert to make someone else happy. But a lot of the time what I hear is, "Well, when I was a teenager, I had this sense that I ought to be Jewish or that I belong Jewish." Or the person says, "I've only dated Jewish men." You start to feel like this is not an accident that this person is here. (emphasis in original)

And so rabbis from all of the denominations may find both justification and joy in facilitating the conversion of the non-Jewish partner in an intermarried couple.[7]

Conversion Requirements

If rabbis are getting much less reticent than they once were about encouraging conversion, have they done anything to make the conversion process easier or more accessible? What do rabbis require of potential converts? A Reform rabbi describes a fairly typical set of requirements for Reform synagogues:

...The basic [requirement] is learning and a significant Jewish education. I prefer to do the learning in a class setting because there is the reaction of other people. On the other hand, the results of people who study with you privately are so astounding — they learn so much and develop such a won-

---

[7] Only about 15% of intermarriages result in a conversion of the non-Jewish spouse to Judaism, according to the 1990 NJPS.

derful feeling for it that it is a terrific way to bring people into the community. In any case, they have to study — and it is an extended period of study. I require them to attend *Shabbat* services twice a month for a period of time. I don't take roll, but I try to pay attention whether they are there or not. They meet with me individually about once a month for six months and we discuss issues and problems and progress. There is a conversion support group for couples which meets monthly when we have enough couples to get a group together...Ultimately they need to join the Temple. They need to commit to being part of the Jewish community.

Then...there is that point where people pass from thinking that they are going to become Jewish and deciding that they are going to become Jewish to feeling Jewish or whatever. They need to get to that point. When we get to the end of the process, it usually takes a year or so. They need to write an essay describing their journey into Judaism. We have a *beit din* in which we primarily discuss the essay. We then go through the ritual aspects. Almost everyone I have converted goes to the *mikvah.* I encourage it. I have had a couple who felt so uncomfortable with it that I didn't insist that they do it. In the case of men, circumcision is something that I urge, but do not require.

A Conservative rabbi describes the process he requires. As one would expect from a Conservative rabbi, he places more emphasis on specific observances, like *Shabbat* and *kashrut*:

I have a whole curriculum — it is what I consider to be the basic elements of a Jewish education. Of course the emphasis is very pragmatic — how to live as a Jew in every circumstance when there is something Jewish to do. So that's a survey of daily practice, *Shabbat,* the cycle of holidays, the life cycle. In addition to that, we do a survey of sacred texts, and study samples of the bible, biblical commentary, the Talmud, some mystical literature, the codes of Jewish law, and so forth. We do a quick survey of Jewish history — a bird's eye view. I try to give some attention to Jewish community and modern

Jewish philosophy. I ask my students to acquire a basic, rudimentary, reading knowledge of Hebrew.

Then I ask them to make the commitments that are required. For me that includes ultimately, or step by step, to become an observant Jew — to observe *Shabbat*, to have a kosher home, to make those commitments, and to become part of the community. And for the Jewish spouse, if there is a Jewish spouse, I ask them to join the congregation right away. Then, of course, assuming that all goes well, then we arrange the conversion itself — circumcision, *mikvah.*

An Orthodox rabbi speaks about the requirements for conversion in somewhat more general terms, and emphasizes the fact that not everyone who starts on the path to conversion makes it to that point:

Generally, if someone does an Orthodox conversion, they have to have a commitment to the Torah, to God, to trying to observe the *mitzvot.* I'm not saying that people have to succeed in observing in every *mitzvah*, because I don't think any of us actually succeeds in that, but the attitude toward trying to observe the *mitzvot* would be, "If I slip and fall, I'm going to brush myself off and try again," and not, "All the *mitzvot* apply to me except this one..."

...You need a course of observance and practice and study...If you work really hard at it, you may be able to do it in somewhat over a year. If you don't work really hard at it, it may never happen. If it's not right for you, it shouldn't happen...All kinds of people start the process. A small percentage of them actually complete that process and convert. Others keep at it for a long time. Others decide at one point or another that it is not for them.

While the Orthodox rabbi emphasizes the amount of hard work conversion takes, Rabbi Henry Cohen (R) represents perhaps a more typical view as he bubbles with delight at the experiences he has had teaching conversion courses:

...There is nothing like teaching Judaism to non-Jews who are on a genuine spiritual search, there is nothing like seeing Judaism fresh, through their eyes, to make one more deeply appreciate the values of our heritage we too often take for granted.

Judaism is not only good for the non-Jews, Cohen seems to say, but it is good for the Jews to see how good it is for the non-Jews.

Preventing "Insincere" Conversions

Of course, not all rabbis view the current trend toward encouraging conversion with such pleasure. With conversion being viewed by so many rabbis and others as a way around the problem of intermarriage, and with conversion requirements being largely at the discretion of each individual rabbi, especially among Reform Jews, some rabbis worry that some conversions might be insincere or *halachically* invalid. The high rate of inter-marriage, in this view, increases the likelihood that many conversions will be conversions of convenience. An Orthodox rabbi describes his attempt to stem the flow of what he sees as these sorts of impermissible conversions:

...What I have been encountering is children of congregants who have intermarried or are contemplating intermarriage. There is a very difficult cycle that takes place. You have a traditional Jewish couple whose child has married someone who is not Jewish, and the parents feel that at this point that they have to do something. They work and work to convince the young couple that the son or daughter-in-law has to have a conversion. They finally get them to a point where they are willing to accept conversion, and then they come to the rabbi. Then I have to break the sad news to them that in 9 out of 10 of those situations it is not a situation where I can do a conversion. It is not motivated, it is not sincere. ...

The Orthodox rabbi explains, further, that he is trying to let us congregants know that he "understands the reality of the social situation, that they may have children who are dating non-Jews and will marry non-Jews, and I am prepared to be a source of understanding of what they are going through." The Orthodox rabbi can provide counsel to pained parents, but he cannot officiate at a conversion he finds to be unmotivated or insincere. And he cannot countenance a conversion that is done merely at the behest of desperate Jewish in-laws.

It is not only Orthodox rabbis who worry about the sincerity of a potential conversion. Some Reform rabbis adopt a "modern application" of the traditional notion that a potential convert should be turned away three times, so that his or her sincerity and determination can be tested. A Reform rabbi explains:

> ...Although I don't do the traditional turning away of somebody three times, my modern application of that is to stress how difficult conversion is. In most cases, it is going to be at least a year. I make it very clear that even though we may decide to start the process now doesn't mean that we are going to finish the process. Anytime along the way they may decide that it is not for them. ...

Another issue confronting rabbis, given the current trend to encourage conversion, is whether or not they can accept the conversions of other denominations. An Orthodox rabbi describes his pain at having to tell a woman that according to *halachic* standards, she was not really Jewish, though she had gone through a conversion process:

> ...It is not an easy issue. One time a person came to me who was very upset. She really felt that she was converted to Judaism — she was converted in a Reform synagogue. She had no *mikvah*, no learning, and no real acceptance. But she really thought that she was Jewish and that is a tragedy.

Another Orthodox rabbi describes a similar situation in which he had to tell a young member of his synagogue that she could not have her *bat mitzvah* there unless she underwent a formal conversion and undertook a commitment to observing *mitzvot:*

> I had a situation where someone came to plan the *bat mitzvah* of her daughter. She said, "I think you might want to know — she's not really my daughter — she's my daughter, but adopted." And the follow up was that she was adopted when they were members of a Reform Temple and no one ever did any kind of immersion ceremony. If they had, it wouldn't have been one that we recognized in an Orthodox *shul* anyway. So I was in the terrible situation of saying — even though I had known her daughter for a long time, and they were involved in the synagogue to some extent — "We are not going to be able to do the *bat mitzvah*, unless there is reason to do a formal Orthodox conversion. And it's unlikely that you are going to be able to do a formal Orthodox conversion unless your lifestyle changes in radical ways." That was an awful moment, but that was what I had to do, at least as I understood it.

The new push toward conversion on the part of some rabbis thus creates an extra, painful burden for other rabbis who fear conversions of convenience, and for those who do not view non-Orthodox conversions as valid. It is as though the harder some rabbis push to open the gates, the more vigorously other rabbis must pull the gates shut. Some congregants will inevitably find themselves caught in the middle, welcomed as honored Jews-by-choice by some, turned away as sadly deceived non-Jews by others.

HOW RABBIS HANDLE CONVERSION

There are a number of ways that rabbis' attitudes and behavior inhibit rather than encourage conversion. Even where intentions are good, and the rabbi believes they are behaving in a proactive and encouraging manner, their language and technique can be counterproductive. Not all rabbis put potential converts off and many can be quite encouraging in both style and substance. But as a whole, interviews indicate that rabbis tend to be more of a barrier than a facilitating presence in bringing potential converts into Judaism.

The first barrier is attitudinal, with most rabbis demanding that the potential convert prove that they want to be Jewish. The potential convert must demonstrate that they are truly committed and eager to become a Jew, usually at the first inquiry or soon into the exploration process. Most rabbis look for proof of sincerity, commitment, and willingness to make sacrifices of time and energy. With some rabbis, the desire to convert to Judaism to accommodate a potential spouse or spouse's family is not proof enough. Although such an act can actually constitute an enormous act of familial faith and responsibility, some rabbis view this reasoning as insincere since the person who is converting does not have a burning desire to become a Jew for some other ideological or theological reasons. Many rabbis view their conversations with potential converts as a testing process, using words and issuing challenges to determine if the person is worthy of conversion or not. It is not clear from the interviews how many pass the test, but it is clear that many rabbis construct an arduous exam before they will engage in the conversion process. Some of this may be tied to the desire to protect their own time, that is, to avoid investing a lot of their professional and psychic energy into someone who is not serious and will abandon the process before completing it. But it appears that most of the motivation comes more from a deep-seated tradition of keeping people at bay rather than helping them along.

An Orthodox rabbi outlines his high standards at the outset for those investigating conversion:

> I am very clear with those that call that the *beit din* will not do an Orthodox conversion unless there is a clear commitment to living an observant lifestyle. *Shabbat* and *Kashrut* become key factors. I tell people that even if I were to agree to take them on as candidates there is no guarantee that the process will culminate in conversion unless this could be demonstrated. A lot of times they don't even know what that means. In many cases, the phone call has them understanding that this is probably not the right way to go, because what they are prepared to commit to is not what I am prepared to accept and it ends there. ...

The interviews reveal a relatively harsh language as rabbis discuss their interaction with potential converts. They often talk about requirements as if they were discussing an entrance exam. They often use the word "insist" rather than explain or encourage. They describe their conversation with a potential convert as an "interview," as if the person were applying for a job or admission. Some require that the potential convert write an essay about themselves, a personal statement that one might find on a college application. The Orthodox rabbi describes his methods regarding potential candidates who, after being given "time to think about what we have discussed," request a meeting:

> I am usually looking for several things when I interview an individual who I think might be a serious candidate for conversion. Motivation and sincerity are the two key factors: what is motivating this person to want to convert and how sincere are they in that motivation.

The road to conversion is long and arduous for many of the potential converts. A statement of interest is often followed by requirements of three months, six months, and a year or more of study, synagogue attendance, learning Hebrew, and other measures to increase the knowledge and ability of the convert to participate in Jewish life. All of these may be extremely useful and important in paving the way for the convert to be an active member of the Jewish community, but is also a great deal to ask of individuals who have no previous experience and whose commitment may grow over time but may be absent at the outset. Sometimes, of course, these requirements are asked of individuals whose Jewish spouses may be less knowledgeable and indeed may be indifferent, or even hostile, to their spouse becoming so involved in Jewish literacy and life. Therefore, a rabbi who insists on an enormous up-front commitment may enter the difficult territory of the Jewish spouse's ambiguous identity. Asking individuals to make a commitment to long-term study, to be certain of why they want to be a Jew, and devotion to Jewish life before they have an understanding of any of these issues is often an oxymoron. Most of these individuals, of course, will not be able to make such a commitment to explain why they are so interested and desirous of being a Jew when they know so little about it. In some ways the initial screening process dooms most potential converts to failure at the outset since requirements of certainty of devotion are demanded before the individual is equipped to do so. An Orthodox rabbi points out how difficult the conversion process can be:

They have to read Hebrew. If someone doesn't read Hebrew, they are left out. We have a class in basic Judaism. These classes are not specifically keyed to converts. We expect them to also come to our bible study class on Monday night. It is a commitment. It is not an easy situation. Conversion requires the following: you have to accept yourself as being a Jew, then there is *mikvah*, and if it is a male there is circumcision.

Few of the interviews revealed any real joy and passion on the part of the rabbi in engaging in a conversion process. Some stated that they felt a great deal of satisfaction, accomplishment and pleasure at the end of the process when someone overcomes all of the hurdles and actually becomes a Jew. Some also have pleasure in the fact that someone made it through, that a person endured all of the testing ground and became a real and committed Jew. But most of the discussions treated the issue as if it were a chore or a problem to be handled: how to deal with the many individuals who are marrying Jewish spouses who may or may not truly be interested in Judaism. Few exhibited enthusiasm for the opportunity to engage in the conversion process, and no one stated that they actively seek converts or view it as part of their ideology to seek out people to help them convert. Most responses were more passive-aggressive, waiting for people to come to them and then responding with one degree of openness or severity or another. For most, conversion was a problem to be dealt with, a better option than an intermarriage, and a better solution to a problem. It was rarely viewed as something positive, that is, the creation of more Jews. Conversion is better than the alternative, but not necessarily a desirable goal. An Orthodox rabbi explains:

> My line usually is, if there is something worth preserving about Judaism, worth handing down to the next generation, then you don't put yourself in a situation where you can't do that — which intermarriage very often is. I also want to maintain the option that if this person you are going with is open to conversion, thinking about conversion. It's not the ideal reason for conversion to Judaism. ...

Some rabbis also charge for the service of conversion. One rabbi, for example, charges twenty dollars an hour during the conversion process. While other professional services may require remuneration, the charging of a fee for the purpose of conversion may seem antithetical to some of the prospective converts. The synagogue and other elements of Jewish life are already filled with fee-for-service components, including synagogue membership, that the idea of paying for a conversion is likely problematic for some of the potential converts, especially where the Jewish spouse is already ambivalent about his or her own identity and connection to the Jewish community.

Most rabbis think they are either being helpful or upholding standards, or both. They are unaware of the harshness of their tone and the dissuasive character of their actions, even when they are trying to be positive.

TEACHING AND PREACHING

Focusing on the Richness of Judaism

In our survey of the actions rabbis take with regard to inter-marriage, we arrive at the action that many rabbis regard to be at the core of their rabbinical practice — teaching. We will focus primarily, of course, on teaching as it relates to intermarriage. It should be noted, however, that rabbis teach in a broad variety of contexts, and about many things that do not directly relate to intermarriage. Some rabbis see their teaching in this widest sense — teaching with no direct allusion to intermarriage — as having the greatest power to prevent intermarriage and Jewish assimilation generally. If Jews come to understand the rich content of Judaism — its wisdom about how to live a good life, its moving history, its poetic languages — Jews will want to stay Jewish. If they fall in love with a non-Jew, they will encourage that person to convert, and will build a Jewish home. If Jews love Judaism, Jewish survival is ensured. Rabbi Charles Lippman (R) expresses such a view:

I believe that the time is overdue for us, and I of course include myself, to teach and learn more about Judaism and

Jewish spirituality. Our concern about intermarriage should be matched by concern that so many know so little about Judaism, that rather than being their "faith," it is all too often only an inconsequential fact of ethnic origin. With renewed emphasis on Jewish teachings and spirituality, I believe that Judaism will better fill the normal human religious needs of our people and of those who choose to associate themselves with us. More Jews, including more who intermarry, will feel that Judaism is something to believe in.

Reiterating the idea that the key to Jewish survival lies in a vital, active, practicing Jewish community, a Reform rabbi describes his work and his considerable confidence about the future:

> ...I'm not worried about Jewish identity for my children or our children collectively here at the synagogue because they see their parents and their community and they are integrated into the language of Jewish life and living. That's all that I can offer them — our love of it and our joy of it.

Like the other rabbis mentioned in Chapter 2 who think that intermarriage has become a scapegoat for more widespread problems of Jewish ignorance and disaffection, the previously interviewed Reform rabbi avoids teaching about intermarriage per se. He focuses on the "love and joy" of Jewish living. While he is a Reform rabbi who does officiate at intermarriages, the spirit of his words is not so different from those of a previously interviewed Orthodox rabbi, whose religious ideology is in many ways worlds away from that of the Reform rabbi. They both stress the value of a rich Jewish life: "The goal of having a vibrant, deep, caring Jewish community is not to avoid intermarriage. It's an end in itself." There are rabbis, however, who find that an *essential* part of their role as teacher and community builder involves discouraging youth from interdating and intermarriage.

Urging Young Jews to Date and Marry Other Jews

In Chapter 2, we mentioned Rabbi Jack Segal's (C) decision to write to the college-age members of his congregation on the subject of intermarriage and interdating, rather than to bring these "extremely delicate" issues up with the congregation at large from the pulpit. Let us examine at some length the text of that letter, where Rabbi Segal describes how interdating can unwittingly, inexorably lead to intermarriage, even among young people who have no intention of marrying non-Jews:

> ...Most students tell me, "Rabbi, you're still living in an ancient generation. You're thinking with the mentality of your generation, not the mentality of our generation. There's nothing wrong with interdating. We're only high school students or college students. Our minds are now centered on our studies, on our professions, and having a good time — but not on marriage. You are overcautious. We are not interested in getting married out of our faith. We're only interested in dating people of other faiths and having a good time with them and broadening our social experiences."
> ...Unfortunately, experience has proven that when emotions become strong, no logical or rational arguments are of any value to young lovers to convince them to terminate the relationship. At that time the relationship has gone beyond "the point of no return." The "critical mass" has been reached — and passed. ...
> ...Very often we think a conversion will eventually take place as a culmination of the Jew dating the non-Jew. It will eventually result in a Jew marrying a Jew. However, very often the non-Jewish partner says, "I thought I could convert, but I cannot convert. I do not believe in Judaism." or "I cannot convert. Why should I? You are not a 'religious Jew' yourself." or "I cannot convert because this would be a dishonest act on my behalf — even though I love you passionately." And due to the fact that emotions and passions have gone beyond "the point of no return," the Jewish partner rationalizes and intel-

lectualizes and says, "It's really not that bad. We both believe in God, in a Supreme Being. This is 1991, not 1891" — and the result is an intermarriage.

Rabbi Segal assumes that his audience starts out with the intention *not* to intermarry. They defend their inter*dating*, according to him, precisely on the grounds that it will not lead to intermarriage. Rabbi Segal's pitch, in this context, is against interdating. He tries to show how the intention to marry a Jew can go awry if the young adult is foolhardy enough to think that he or she can date non-Jews without falling in love with them.

Other rabbis, teaching in other contexts, find that they cannot make the assumption Rabbi Segal makes. Their students, they find, start out believing that intermarriage is fine, and interdating all the more so. In this context, the rabbi has to try to come up with a rationale against intermarriage. It is not an easy pitch to make, a Reform rabbi reports, describing her work with the teenage students in her confirmation class:

> ...The most shocking repeated sentiment to me is the notion that we're prejudiced because we don't want intermarriage...Half of them [the students] come from homes where one partner isn't Jewish, so how can we even suggest this [that we don't want intermarriage]

Accused of being prejudiced for opposing intermarriage, needing to walk a tightrope so as to avoid insulting the parents or their students, the Reform rabbi nonetheless tries to make the case for inmarriage to her students:

> ...It's difficult. We talk a lot about history and building a home that's based in one faith, and why that's important. We have couples speak to them who have gone through the pain of intermarriage and are now resolved — maybe because one partner has now converted — that's real helpful. But they [the students] don't care; they don't hear that [intermarriage

involves a lot of pain]. All they know is they like this person or that person and every time you suggest that it's difficult to have a home with two faiths, someone in the room says, well, "My mom and dad have that, and we're doing fine."

...We have taught them so well, out of the sixties, that everyone is treated equal and we're all God's children, and we're all beautiful human beings, why should we only marry someone who is Jewish. I think we do a much better job if we teach them that there is a Jewish way of looking at the world from the beginning, and that sharing that world view with someone else enhances a relationship, as opposed to trying to teach them that marrying someone who doesn't have that world view is bad. It's hard.

Here, she has found a way to try to temper her expression of what her students often interpret to be her "racism." She tries to promote the joy and power of finding a mate who shares a Jewish world view rather than focusing exclusively on what she sees as the negative aspects of intermarriage.

A Conservative rabbi like many other rabbis we spoke with, echoes the idea that Jews, young Jews especially, see an anti-inter-marriage position as racist. The Conservative rabbi does what he can to counter that charge, but the despair with which he talks about the situation indicates that stressing the problems of inter-marriage runs deeply against the grain — even in his fairly obser-vant, tight-knit Conservative congregation:

...The kids, by the time they reach [confirmation] age, to them, to oppose intermarriage is to be a racist. That's their point of view...Every Jewish character on television is involved with a non-Jewish sexual partner or marital partner, and the American democratic idea is that you are not allowed to make important distinctions like who you are going to marry on the basis of race, religion or anything like that. So these kids have that idea.

The issue almost always comes up because as part of their confirmation they give talks on contemporary issues. So naturally that is one that they tend to be thinking of...It is always so distressing to me to see how their attitudes are absolutely uninformed by any kind of Jewish point of view on this. It doesn't constrain me because I don't have any problem telling them, "Look, I really disagree with your ideas." But it is still kind of daunting to encounter how widespread those ideas are.

Having come to believe through difficult experience that speaking against intermarriage from the pulpit causes much more pain, turmoil and alienation than it promotes understanding, this Conservative rabbi has stopped delivering sermons on the subject. Other rabbis do, however, use their pulpits to try to persuade their congregants of the dangers of intermarriage and to promote the power of inmarriage.

Urging Parents to Promote inmarriage

One strategy adopted by some rabbis is to employ sermons to try to get parents to take a more active role in teaching their children the importance of marrying a Jew. In a *Rosh Hashanah* sermon entitled "Ten Things Jewish Parents Don't Say Enough to their Children," Rabbi Jack Moline's (C) "number three" statement is "I expect you to marry a Jew." Rabbi Moline asks:

> ...How is it that we open a savings account for college when a baby is born and put dollars in it faithfully but we consider it too soon to discuss married life until a kid is already suspicious of his parents? How is it we don't hesitate to discuss good touching and bad touching with pre-schoolers, but when they play bride and groom we don't ask, "but where's the *chupah*? where's the *ketubah*?"...
> ...A clear and articulate message on your rules for interdating is essential long before your child has her first kiss. I don't think it ever too early to make a distinction between friendship and love. ...

Teaching the value of a Jewish marriage should be a natural, everyday, explicit part of child rearing, according to Rabbi Moline, and he urges parents to rise to the task.

Emphasizing the Dangers of Intermarriage

Rabbi Moline and others concentrate on teaching the positive aspects of marrying a Jew — being able to share one faith, getting to take part in traditional Jewish acts, like signing a *ketubah* and getting married under a *chupah*. He and other rabbis and others also find room in their teaching to take a more negative approach. In addition to teaching the positive aspects of Judaism, they want to let teenagers and unmarried adults know that married life with a non-Jew will be difficult. And so as we have seen, the Reform rabbi on the one hand finds it "real helpful" when intermarried couples speak to her confirmation class about "the pain of inter-marriage." On the other hand, she admits that the negative side of the argument is hard to sell, that students are not open to the idea that "marrying someone who doesn't have that [Jewish] world view is bad."

Rabbi Moline, in his sermon quoted earlier, picks up the neg-ative part of the argument:

> ...We must be honest with the intermarried couple about con-sequences. They should know that intermarriages are twice as likely to end in divorce as inmarriages. They should know that their children are unlikely to marry within the Jewish faith and even less likely to produce Jewish offspring. They should know that, like the man in the Torah reading today, they and their children will be the source of confusion for the mainstream Jewish community, and that such confusion may be interpreted by their children as rejection, though it is not meant to be. They should know that at life-cycle events — *brit milah* or naming, *bar* or *bat mitzvah*, marriage, burial — there may be obstacles to full family participation.

In this passage, Rabbi Moline seeks to warn young people, or to have their parents warn them, that life in an intermarriage is tough. But hanging onto this negative message is tough, itself, just as it is hard for rabbis to maintain a steady hold on their desire to greet intermarriage with both negative social sanctions and support. Here, Rabbi Moline's "honest" warning remains highly indirect. Where and when does Rabbi Moline imagine this sort of frank talk taking place? Who does he think should take on the job of telling a married couple that their marriage is highly likely to end in divorce? Who is going to tell them, face to face, that "their children are a source of confusion"?

We know, from an earlier point in Rabbi Moline's sermon, that "after the fact," he is in favor of marriage, after the fact, "the business at hand is creating a loving and stable marriage." And so it seems unlikely that *he* would engage in the honesty he advocates here and say to any given married couple, "Your marriage will likely end in divorce." The sermon advocates an abstract, indirect message of foreboding and disapproval; but from his other words, we understand that the rabbi would find it uncomfortable and distasteful to send this negative message to a real, particular couple.

Sending Warnings While Teaching Acceptance

Note again how a passive turn in the sermon's language serves to send indirectly a message of exclusion that Rabbi Moline could not countenance sending directly. He warns, on the one hand, in the passive voice, that the intermarried couple must realize that various unnamed people may distance themselves from intermarried couples, that "there may be obstacles to full family participation" in various life-cycle events. But later in the sermon, talking about his policies and his congregation, he energetically rolls out the welcome mat:

We must make it abundantly clear that intermarried families are welcome in our communities and the resources of Jewish life are available to them in the hopes of enhancing their own Jewish lives. No one will be turned away from worship, from learning, from communal celebration, from counseling or consoling.

The obstacles have been forgotten. And so one might walk away from this sermon, just as one might walk away from a discussion with a rabbi about his or her willingness to officiate at an intermarriage ceremony, confused. Rabbi Moline's sermon, which we have just reviewed at some length, is one of the most articulate of a very common genre. But we picture a congregant walking away from such a sermon, having difficulty sorting it all out:

Okay, now, he thinks intermarriage is a shame, but he also fully respects it. He can't officiate, but he knows great rabbis who do. He wants us to join the synagogue, and we will be very welcome, but we should know that there are some things we will not be allowed to do. Some of his best friends have intermarried, and some of his favorite members of the congregation are non-Jews, but he did not go to their weddings. He hopes that I will not marry someone non-Jewish, but if I do, what really matters is that I raise the kids Jewish. But I should remember that not everyone will agree that the kids actually are Jewish.

It is a great deal for anyone to remember. Little wonder that some rabbis refrain from giving sermons on the subject, and turn to other forums to express their views.

COUNSELING

Urging Acceptance of the Rabbi's Position: Dealing with Parents

Depending upon the communities in which they work, rabbis are likely to encounter different sorts of distress on the part of parents of young couples who are about to intermarry. In some contexts, the parents' discontent is focused on their congregational rabbi, who refuses to officiate at their child's wedding. Having already come to terms themselves with the idea that their child is marrying a non-Jew, the parents express anger at the rabbi, who seems to be putting a damper on what should be a joyous occasion. A Reform rabbi explains this kind of counseling situation, which perhaps must be better understood as the rabbi's inescapable public relations work:

> [Some] families get angry. [They] were not angry when they agreed with you before their child ended up in the situation. [But now] they become very angry, and they start the bargaining: "Can we have an *aufrufin?*" I say no. So you get into that. They say, "Look, you won't let us have the wedding, now we can't have the *aufrufin...*"
>
> They just want you to do the service...They want you just to do the show. Because they have accepted it already...I try to be as friendly as I can. Most of them will accept that, but some get very uptight.

In this rabbi's community, as he says, parents have come to expect that their children will marry non-Jews, "they have accepted it already." And they want others to go along with that reality, to put on a show of a Jewish wedding.

Working in a similar community, another Reform rabbi enjoys having an opportunity to explain to congregation members his understanding of the officiation issue — many of whom are inclined, at first, to see his refusal to officiate at intermarriages as insensitive and uncaring:

> If someone wants to know what I do and why, first of all I want them to know what I *do* do, and not just what I don't do. [There are many things I do]...in terms of giving the same freedom of conscience to other members of the clergy the same freedom that I have, blessing people in the sanctuary before the wedding, allowing them to be married here under certain circumstances... And then I would explain where my position comes from, which is essentially a two-pronged thing. One is my own sense of what I as a rabbi am empowered to do by the tradition as interpreted by my movement, and the second thing is the aspect of this in which I am trying to function both as an effective rabbi for my congregation and as an effective parent for my children. And not to give a mixed message.
>
> I try to explain that...I didn't become a rabbi to hurt people. That's not my aim; it's the opposite. But this is who I am, and this is where I am coming from. And it's not personal, it's not a judgment on the marriage or the couple or the actions of their life or their choices. It's a decision that is not about them so much as it is about me, even though it obviously affects them in some way. I think for most people, just having a chance to hear that is ameliorating of some of the antipathy that this can arouse.

Reform rabbis who do not officiate at intermarriages clearly must put considerable effort into trying to repair fences with congregants — both young couples and their parents — who find their position intolerant or hopelessly behind the times. It is a kind of repair work that, as one Reform rabbi told us, demands considerable "technique." And as we have seen, the need to engage in such repair can be a considerable burden to the rabbi, shocked at finding him or herself, in a Reform rabbi's words, "disliked, attacked and criticized for taking a position that is so thoroughly authentic within the Jewish tradition."

Intervention or Pre-Marriage Counseling

In other communities, of course, rabbis are expected to oppose intermarriage, and are enlisted as a source of support by parents grieving at their child's choice of a partner. Some rabbis, approached by congregants with the news that a young adult member of the family plans to marry a non-Jew, will try, if possible, to intervene. An Orthodox rabbi explains:

> If I have a relationship with the child, I am able to sit down and talk with them and on occasion I have been able to change the situation around. The more educated the kid is the more chance you have of getting Jewish guilt to come out. Again in many cases you hear — well, my parents aren't Jewish except that they were born Jewish.

Most of the rabbis to whom we spoke assume that there is no use in trying "change the situation around." Nonetheless, many rabbis appreciate a chance to talk to a couple that is considering intermarriage. A Conservative rabbi — like some of the rabbis we noted in the "Enunciating the Dangers of Intermarriage" section — uses the counseling opportunity to push the couple to think about the potential complications of intermarriage:

> If I know someone in the congregation who is planning to marry someone who is not Jewish, I try to make an effort to initiate a time to get together. I do not try to dissuade them from getting married. I do not try to persuade them to convert. I do tell them that they have to deal with some real issues and they are going to come up in the marriage. I tell them that they have to learn to negotiate issues throughout their life. ...

Though he understands that a couple that has decided to get married will get married no matter what he says, he wants couples to anticipate some of the problems they might encounter.

Reiterating, along with other Conservative rabbis, that he does not expect to change anyone's mind, this Conservative rabbi likes to have a chance to talk to couples to let them know that they will be welcome back in his synagogue after the wedding:

> One thing that I have strict instructions to my secretary and all the staff of the synagogue is that if somebody calls don't say over the phone that the rabbi doesn't do intermarriages. I have talked to many, many couples and I can't say that I have changed anybody's mind, but I at least let them know that the door is open...We want [them] to feel that this is a place that [they] can come.

Echoing his message, but focusing a bit more on concrete actions that a couple might take to become more involved with Judaism, another Conservative rabbi does his best to lay out an enticing array of ways to get involved in Jewish learning and synagogue life:

> If [an intermarried couple] lives in my community, I want them to know who I am and where the synagogue is. I immediately put them on my mailing list. I want to show them the opportunities where they can meet with us and to tell them about the Basic Judaism class which meets in my office every other Sunday. The class in Jewish Ethics meets every Saturday morning before services. I want to also tell them that where they live there may be neighbors from the synagogue and [to ask whether] they are comfortable with those people calling on them. If they want to study, they need to tell me what they are interested in. If in fact they tell me that they want to study about Judaism, there is the Lehrhaus. The key to that is that they will not be alone. ...

While most rabbis feel that they must strive to be supportive to young adults embarking on an intermarriage, many are also called upon to support the Jewish parents of such couples, some of whom may feel grief at their child's decision.

Supporting Parents in Grief

Recognizing that parents with intermarried children have begun to be a significant subset of many congregations, some rabbis have initiated support groups for such people. A Conservative rabbi comments on one such group at his synagogue for "parents who feel in danger of their kids getting intermarried":

> ...It has been a good group. It hasn't solved anyone's problems, but it has given people a forum to be able to talk and share their feelings. ...

Other rabbis have found themselves taking a more active role facilitating communication between parent and adult child. In some such situations, a rabbi who strongly opposes intermarriage might ironically find him or herself urging a particular couple of parents to try to be more accepting. A Conservative rabbi describes one such situation involving one of the most active families in his congregation:

> ...The kids had all been extremely active, had all gone to Israel, etc., etc. The boy went off to college and fell in love with a non-Jewish woman. The parents would not let the girl in the house, were totally opposed to it, just completely. So...I would counsel, try to get the parents to relax a little and not disown the kid, and I tried to get the kid to see why his parents would react so strongly.
>
> With the couple, the boy and his non-Jewish spouse, I tried to explain to them both that I could understand why they were hurt at what the parents were doing, but to try to see why it was so important. I tried to make it clear to the young woman that I would support them if she ever wanted to convert to Judaism — because the parents would not. You know, very often the parents [think that] conversion is not good enough. I get that a lot, which really complicates my job, because officially the Conservative movement takes the posi-

tion that when there is intermarriage, or when a Jew falls in love with a non-Jew, the best bet is conversion. But the parents don't always accept that — especially if there are racial issues.

The parental strategies described here by this Conservative rabbi, actions that parents might once have taken to express disapproval at their child dating a non-Jew — not letting the partner into their home, threatening to disown their child — have become extremely rare among the congregants of the rabbis we studied. As the rabbi's recounting suggests, however, there are some communities in which parents do wish that they had some recourse, some way to reverse their child's decision about whom to marry. In such cases, a rabbi might find him or herself counseling the parent to accept what appears to be a *fait accompli.*

In this context, it will be valuable to consider at some length portions of a letter sent by an Orthodox rabbi to a woman who wrote him, seeking his advice on how to respond to her son's relationship to a non-Jewish woman. In the letter, the Orthodox rabbi urges the woman to do what she can do retain or regain a good relationship with her son, and to recognize that she does not have the power to change his mind about his choice of a romantic partner. The Orthodox rabbi's letter reads, in part, as follows:

I feel, as I read your letter, the depth of your sincere desire to see your son married to a Jewish woman, and indeed, himself an observant Jew. I share this desire, for your son and for other Jews in America. However, each Jew reaches his or her own conclusions about how to, or whether to, observe Judaism. That seems to be how G-d made the world. We do not decide for others. At best, we who do try to observe succeed in setting beautiful examples; at best, when other Jews begin their search for Judaism, we appear to them as good resources. When we have not been asked for our opinion, and still tell other Jews to behave differently, we risk being dismissed or despised. Indeed, the Rabbis of the Talmud, may their memories serve as a blessing, taught this.

Rabbi Eliezer ben Simon said, "Just as it is a *mitzvah* to say a word which would be heard, so it is a *mitzvah* not to say a word which would not be heard." Rabbi Abba said, "An obligation, as it says, 'Do not reprove a disobedient one, lest he hate you; reprove the wise, and he will love you'." (Proverbs 9:8). (Yevamot 65a)

Your letter implies that you have already become somewhat estranged from your son, who does not want to hear your evaluation of his religious life or his choice of mate. It seems likely, based on what you have written to me, that further advice would only inspire him to further reduce his relationship with you. Not knowing the situation first-hand, I can only rely on what I understand from your letter. Still, it seems clear to me that you stand a better chance of having some relationship with him, and perhaps some positive influence, if you don't give up hope of having any influence. Then write to him, or call, about all manner of other things, and absolutely never bring up this subject. Rabbi Abba said it is an obligation not to say a word which will not be heard.

There was a time, not long ago, when excommunication, the Herem, served as a real weapon. The Jews who opposed intermarriage could cut off that small minority who intermarried, and so discourage other Jews from following their path. A painful therapy, costly in each individual case, it made sense in the aggregate. Now, when a large minority, if not an absolute majority, of the Jews in America do intermarry, it makes no sense for us to try to cut them off.

Now we must befriend them, and speak gently with them, and try to maintain our relationship with them. Perhaps someday we will have the opportunity to say a word which would be heard, if not about this *mitzvah*, perhaps about another. Perhaps the occasion to speak will never arise. As the Talmud records Rabbi Shimon HaEmsoni saying, in a slightly different context, "In the same way that I have earned reward for teaching, so I have earned reward for refraining." (Pesahim 23b).

May the One who wipes away the tears from all eyes bring comfort to you, a mother in Israel.

The Orthodox rabbi reiterates the notion we have encountered earlier, that American Jews who oppose intermarriage are not in a position — except in the most insulated communities — to cut off Jews who do intermarry. His letter is perhaps most noteworthy for the eloquence with which it expresses what is the "bottom line" of the majority of rabbis when they console themselves and others about the prevalence of intermarriage: They wish it were not so, but it is so.

DEFINING THE ROLE OF INTERMARRIED JEWS AND NON-JEWS IN THE SYNAGOGUE

Given the prevalence of intermarriage, it follows that all of the various life-cycle events and many regular synagogue functions — not only wedding ceremonies — are frequently affected by the presence of non-Jews in Jewish families and synagogues. Nearly every rabbi with whom we spoke has had to help guide synagogue policy with regard to the participation of intermarried Jews and their non-Jewish partners in the ritual, educational and administrative life of the synagogue. The range of practices is as wide as one might imagine in light of earlier discussions in this chapter. For the most extreme among the Orthodox, even the *Jewish* partner of an intermarriage has no legitimate role in synagogue life, and should not be numbered among the *minyan*. For the most liberal of the congregation, non-Jews are full members of the synagogue, and may be restricted (formally or informally) only from a very few public functions, such as serving as synagogue president or being called for an *aliyah* to the Torah.

The Status of a Jew in an Intermarriage

Between those two extremes, of course, there is quite a bit of middle ground, and rabbis work with their congregants and board members in staking out the territory. Let us examine a few examples of the ways rabbis handle issues of the involvement of intermarried Jews and non-Jews in the synagogue. One Orthodox rabbi we spoke with told of a stir which had been created when one of the synagogue elders — one of the men who normally had a prominent, honorific role during High Holiday services, married a non-Jewish woman (in his second marriage). There was considerable feeling on the part of members of the congregation that it was inappropriate for someone in an intermarriage to be granted high honors on the High Holidays. So the rabbi engineered what he hoped was a tactful way of redistributing all of these sorts of honors, including the one that would normally have gone to this particular elder. A far cry from ostracism, this community's reaction to a Jewish man who had married a non-Jewish woman nonetheless entailed a palpable demotion in status of that man.

Such a story, where the focus is on what limits might be placed on the synagogue participation of an intermarried Jew is rare among the rabbis we studied. A Conservative rabbi did note, "Someone who was married to a non-Jew I wouldn't be comfortable with as President of my *shul.* There are limits." A Reform rabbi, on the other hand, reported "I would say of our recent presidents I can't think of any who had a Jewish partner." Indeed, in most synagogues the only questions have to do with the role of non-Jews in synagogue life.

The Role of Non-Jews in Synagogue Life

The rabbis find the question of how to include non-Jews in synagogue life is particularly vexing because the non-Jews in

question are not just some random non-Jews, not just hypotheti-
cal non-Jews, not just one-time non-Jewish visitors — they are
the family members of Jews, many of whom have woven their
own lives into the life of the synagogue community, albeit without becoming Jewish themselves. Viewing non-Jews of this sort as
constituting a new category, a Conservative rabbi proposes a formal recognition of their status:

> For the record, there should be a third category of person.
> There are Jews, Christians (non-Jews), and then something
> like fellow traveler — someone who is not Jewish *halachical-
> ly*, but who has certain rights as somebody who is truly par-
> ticipating in the life of the Jewish community.

Rabbi Fred Reiner (R) finds precedent for according such a
status, as he explains in a *Yom Kippur* sermon:

> ...The rabbis distinguished among different types of *gerim*.
> One was a *ger toshav*, or a partial proselyte, a person who lived
> among the Jews, but did not formally convert. Such a person
> was considered "one of the family," an honest seeker of truth
> who enjoyed many rights in the Jewish community. If our
> doors are open, we thus have the precedent for bringing these
> sojourners into our midst. They are not temporary, nor
> aliens, nor simply residing in our midst. No, they are our hus-
> bands and wives, our daughters and sons. They are our fami-
> ly, and we must make a place for them in the covenant we
> share with God. ...

Short of formally "making a place" for non-Jews in the
covenant, short of defining such a status as *ger toshav* or "fellow
traveler," rabbis struggle in a daily way with how to include non-
Jews in synagogue life, while somehow maintaining a visible distinction between Jews and non-Jews. The distinctions have
become hard to draw.

A Conservative rabbi lays out with some bittersweet humor the questions regarding participation of non-Jews in the synagogue:

> Our congregation has issues. On the one hand it wants to be welcoming. On the other hand, it has got the *halacha* thing. On the other hand, how can you let a non-Jew go up to the *bimah*. On the other hand, can the non-Jewish partner be a member of the synagogue? What do you do about patrilineal descent?

Another Conservative rabbi's congregation has faced these same questions, as he describes:

> ...Our by-laws say something like "anyone professing to be Jewish" [can be a synagogue member] — it is very vague. There was a big to-do this year...I felt very strongly that if you are Jewish you are Jewish and if not you shouldn't be a member. I dropped my opposition because we felt it was not a smart campaign. It was an issue that would cause a lot of bitterness in the congregation and a lot of young families would be hurt by it. I felt I should just leave well enough alone.
>
> Many people went around saying, "Look, what if one of these non-Jews runs for president?" And I said, "Look — if they are crazy enough to want to become president of the synagogue they can have it."
>
> Currently our only limitation for non-Jewish partners are ritual honors...At a *bar/bat mitzvah*, I have the non-Jewish parent come up and help with the *tallit* and do a parent's prayer with the spouse and do all kinds of readings, but not touching the Torah.

This gives some sense of the sorts of accommodations at which various synagogues have arrived. In this rabbi's synagogue, despite his convictions to the contrary, non-Jews can be members. Other members have to rely on hope and trust that none of them will be "crazy enough" to want to be president. Non-Jews are excluded from certain kinds of ritual honors, but do participate actively in many parts of the religious services.

Participation of Non-Jewish Parents in Bar and Bat Mitzvah Ceremonies

The participation of non-Jews comes up, of course, with regard to almost any life-cycle event. Many of the rabbis we spoke with, for example, will preside at funeral services, if requested, for non-Jewish family members of synagogue members. *B'nai mitzvah* are the most prominent of the other life-cycle events, so we examine here how various rabbis incorporate non-Jewish parents into those ceremonies.

One way that rabbis have found around particular sticky ritual matters is to avoid having non-Jews say things in Hebrew, and to supply them with fairly innocuous English readings. A Reform rabbi describes how he has sorted these matters out during *bar* and *bat mitzvah* ceremonies when there is a non-Jewish parent involved:

> ...There are certain things a non-Jewish parent cannot do. There is very little. [They do not say] any blessing that says "*asher kidshanu b'mitzvotav*" "who sanctified us by the commandments" — they were not [sanctified by the commandments]. And the other "*asher bachar banu*" "who has chosen us." When you have the *kiddush*, before the Friday night *bar mitzvah*, the blessing says "*asher bachar banu*," "God chose us." So, many times we have the student read the Hebrew, while the father reads the English that has nothing to do with it.
>
> For Torah blessings, the non-Jewish parent cannot do it, but they can stand by, if they want to. Very few have asked for that, or care really. But we allow the non-Jewish parent to speak to the student. If we have non-Jewish grandparents they can come up and help open the ark door and march around with us and the Torah, if they are willing.

Another Reform rabbi, similarly, has prepared a statement for a non-Jewish parent to read to his or her child at the *bar/bat mitzvah*:

> I have a statement that I have the mother or father read when the child comes from a intermarriage. "I am proud to present my (son or daughter). I am pleased that he/she is following the path of beautiful and noble tradition. May he/she continue to grow in good health with the love of our family. I thank God for keeping us in life and bringing us all together in happiness." They are so pleased to participate. They can hold the Torah and walk around with us.

It is easy to see why a rabbi would be happy to find ways for a non-Jewish parent to participate in his/her child's *bar/bat mitzvah*. Many rabbis said to us something to the following effect — "Look, often it's the non-Jewish parent who has brought the child up as a Jew." Given such a situation, excluding that parent from public participation in a *bar/bat mitzvah* would be especially painful. We can see the tension in the following comment of a Conservative rabbi, leader of a fairly traditional synagogue. His first impulse is to express a firm stand, severely limiting the public participation of non-Jews in the synagogue:

> A non-Jew in our congregation can't take part in the service in a public way. They can be present, but they can't read any part of the service or anything.

But he immediately follows up this statement with a softening, especially for the case of *bar* and *bat mitzvah*:

> What we do do occasionally when we have a *bar/bat mitzvah* — sometimes the parents speak. If a non-Jewish parent wants to be part of that, we allow them to do that.

Other Programmatic Initiatives — Outreach and Inreach

Facing the reality of high levels of intermarriage, many rabbis have become involved in various programmatic initiatives, which have come to be referred to collectively as "outreach." These programs include those sponsored by national movements and also locally-designed projects. There is the Reform Movement's Gateways to Judaism program, targeted at unaffiliated interfaith families; in it, groups of 4-6 families meet monthly to learn about Jewish life traditions and customs. There are interfaith *havurot* sponsored by individual Reform synagogues, where groups consisting of families or individuals come monthly to socialize, to study or celebrate together. There are discussion groups, couples workshops, newsletters, all aimed specifically at issues confronting members of intermarriages.

Further, each synagogue almost invariably offers various programs which are open to the in-married as well as the intermarried — but which are promoted specifically in informational packets aimed at the intermarried. These often include some kind of Saturday or Sunday morning programming for parents and small children — usually combining teaching about holidays with stories, songs, arts and crafts. Many synagogues offer a monthly program on Friday night called "*Tot Shabbat*," also aimed at young children and parents, often including dinner and singing. Some of the synagogues offer parenting workshops, and many sponsor "Introduction to Judaism" classes, where both non-Jews and Jews are welcome. And of course, rabbis offer private counseling sessions to intermarried couples who are trying to negotiate their religious practices and understandings — this, too, falls under the rubric of "outreach."

Most of the Reform rabbis in this study voiced considerable enthusiasm about their participation in various outreach programs. Rabbi Alexander Schindler, former president of the Union

of American Hebrew Congregations (UAHC), and a chief archi-
tect and advocate of the Reform movement's outreach efforts, sets
the tone for most Reform rabbis on this matter. In his 1991
Presidential Address to the UAHC General Assembly, he argues
that outreach not only serves to attract non-Jews who might be
open to more involvement in Judaism, but also engages Jews who
have become alienated to Judaism:

> Ultimately, *Outreach means inspiring a firmer embrace of
> Judaism within us all*: among the intermarried and the con-
> verted and the unconverted, yes, but also among the born-
> and-bred Jews, the unaffiliated and the marginally affiliated
> who enter and leave our Temples as through a revolving door.
> In this sense, our educational enterprise in its totality is one
> great conversionary effort, for while the factors that deter the
> born Jew and the non-Jewish marriage partner may be differ-
> ent for each, the gulf is no less wide and perhaps even more
> yawning for the born-but-alienated Jew. (emphasis in origi-
> nal)

Rabbi Marcia A. Zimmerman (R), picks up on this theme.
Noting in a *Yom Kippur* sermon that she spends half of her time
as a rabbi doing "outreach," she clearly finds great joy in her work,
in large part because of the way in which her outreach work
touches "born Jews":

> Interfaith couples are the fastest growing constituency in our
> community. And when they come into my study, they are
> struggling with the meaning of religion in their lives. Often
> times it is precisely because the born Jewish partner is with
> someone not Jewish that brings them back to Judaism. Often
> it is the difficult questions asked by the non-Jewish partner
> that makes the born Jew return to study and begin regular
> Jewish observance. Witnessing interfaith couples work to find
> a harmony of religion brings out the real and important
> issues for religious identity, choice of religious observance
> and commitment that I wish all adult Jews would struggle
> with.

In a 1991 *Rosh Hashanah* sermon, finally, Rabbi Howard A. Berman enthusiastically lauds what he sees as the incredible success of his synagogue's program:

> The majority of Outreach couples who continue to live in Chicago after their weddings, and many who move considerable distances away, have remained members of this congregation, and many have continued their Jewish affiliation in other places. Many have taken active roles in all aspects of temple life — in our worship, in our study and in our community service. A remarkable proportion have risen to the ranks of leadership in Sinai — three of our current Officers, and five more of our Temple Trustees are alumni of Outreach!

Rabbi Berman's sermon does not make clear — probably intentionally so — if the Outreach alumni to whom he refers are the born-Jewish members of the intermarried couple, formerly non-Jews who have since converted to Judaism, or non-Jews who remain so. From some perspectives, that does not matter — the point is there are energetic people working hard to foster life at the synagogue. From other perspectives, there would be considerable chagrin if it is the case that that synagogue's board is largely peopled by non-Jews. One also might be alarmed, rather than pleased, that couples who move considerable distances away from Rabbi Berman's synagogue retain their membership there — for what does that imply about their regular attendance at a synagogue? In a word — it is hard to tell, from such testimonials, to what extent outreach programs encourage non-Jews to become Jewish, or foster rich Jewish lives on the part of those who are born Jewish.

For such reasons and others, it should be noted that not all rabbis share Rabbi Berman's enthusiasm for outreach programs. They worry about resources being spent on programs for people who will not end up joining the community, and they would rather nurture the health of what they sometimes call the "committed core." There is a difference in emphasis, and at the end of the day, a rabbi has to decide how and with whom he or she will spend her time. A Conservative rabbi strives to focus his efforts on the already-committed, or at least, those already present in his synagogue:

> It's nice and good that people are doing outreach. I don't think that's my job. I think I'm the one whose job it is to do inreach. If you look at the demographic figures what you see is a community disappearing at the peripheries, but it still has a pretty coherent core. And I think that's basically who belongs to my congregation, people in the core. I see my job more as protecting that core than going out and getting peo-ple...I am very worried that we will get too involved in reach-ing out, and there will be nobody left at the center.
>   ...You have to make an effort to link Jews up, or link their souls up to Judaism again. So the people might be committed, they might show up, their bodies might be here. They might have some kind of ethnic or cultural tie or just habit that brings them here. But that's not strong enough, that's not going to last another generation. They really need something stronger, something more meaningful if they are still going to be around, if they are not going to become part of the periph-ery that is peeling away from the outer layers of the Jewish people. And so that's what I do.

These behaviors both evolve from and inform programmatic direction. The next section discusses what rabbis recommend for the community.

WHAT DO RABBIS RECOMMEND?

Rabbis' feelings about intermarriage inspire them or empow-er them to offer a variety of actions, strategies and tactics to deal with the phenomenon. Approaches can be classified as theoreti-cal, institutional and programmatic. The theoretical, or perhaps philosophical/theological realm, offers a framework where ideas, suggestions and recommendations should guide the rabbinic actions toward institutions, individuals and families. Rabbis have a number of ideas about policy direction for the Jewish community, for their own congregations and for their individual actions in dealing with the issue of intermarriage. They collectively view the problem much more broadly than whether or not they should perform intermarriages or whether or not intermarried couples should be allowed to join synagogues. While there are various views on these subjects, they also have a broad range of ideas on how to approach the issue of intermarriage on a broader communal basis.

The data in this section come from a self-administered mail questionnaire given to Northern California rabbis in 1995, and includes a cross-section of Orthodox, Conservative, Reform and Reconstructionist rabbis. The answers are confidential and anonymous, and therefore attribution is not given to any particular rabbi for any particular response.

Most rabbis are keenly aware of the political character of the Jewish community. Many recognize the need for personal activism as individuals. Furthermore, many may also understand the need for the synagogue to be an active institutional force in the Jewish community. A number of institutional and structural suggestions are made by rabbis as strategies for dealing with the issue of intermarriage. Among those who embrace the outreach/integration ideology, some rabbis advocate insuring that the by-laws of the synagogue are "sensitive to non-Jewish roles in the synagogue." They believe that the constitutional structure of the synagogue needs to provide mechanisms for the active participation of non-Jews, either as members, participants in worship services or as volunteers in lay roles, including serving on committees or as officers of the institution. On the other hand, those who advocate prevention strategies argue that the synagogue must maintain standards, serving as a Jewish institution for

Jewish constituencies. Therefore non-Jews can only participate once they cease to be non-Jews, that is, they convert formally to Judaism. On the one hand, some believe that if they open the institutional door they will produce Jews by osmosis, while others believe that only active maintenance of strict standards will provide enough inducement to those who are serious or potentially serious about being Jews. If they want to participate enough, some argue, they will actively engage in the ritual of conversion. Some argue that they strengthen the institution through outreach and others that they maintain the integrity of the institution by not "watering down" its standards. Both sides recognize the important role of the institution. The internal structure of the synagogue becomes a key playing field for the ideologies of outreach/integration versus prevention. Rabbis are by no means alone in their expression of these varying ideologies. They reflect splits within the congregations themselves where some factions argue for inclusiveness while others argue for more rigid standards. Both have the same goal in mind, the maintenance of the Jewish core, but are clearly on opposite ends of the strategic spectrum of how to achieve group cohesion.

For example, one rabbi calls for a "preventive medicine" campaign that includes hands-on family programming for Jewish living, including *Shabbat, Aliyot, Pesach* and other holiday celebrations to be performed in the *shul* and in the home by having members interchange homes and active celebrations among congregants organized at the synagogue. Another rabbi expands upon this concept by calling for a mentoring program within the synagogue with those who are knowledgeable and active to make a two-year commitment to mentor other families, both in-married and intermarried, in the rituals, learning and activities of Jewish life. A strong Jewish identity, they believe, will either bind some individuals to the Jewish community, recruit others or prevent others from leaving. Making Jewish life manageable, attractive, relevant, accessible, interesting and so on, are seen as the chief strategies for preservation and therefore prevention of inter-marriage.

Others advocate peer groups and friendship circles, specifi-cally in the form of *havurot* for intermarried couples. Couples may participate in programs that are written and designed for them and by them that specifically address the intellectual, famil-ial and social needs of intermarried couples. The assumption is that intermarried couples will feel more comfortable around one another, that non-Jewish spouses can provide a community of support for one another, and that those who participate in these programs will not be embarrassed by either their differences or their lack of familiarity with Jewish life. Of course, in-married couples may be just as unfamiliar, but the philosophy behind spe-cific programs and structures for intermarried couples is the commonly held belief that intermarried couples will be more comfortable in circles that include more people like themselves.

Another set of strategies calls for efforts to reduce costs and other barriers to synagogue participation. For example, some rab-bis advocate sending children of intermarried couples to religious school for one year without membership. The family pays only a registration fee. They argue that these programs must be adver-tised in the non-Jewish press as well as the Jewish newspapers to reach those who are less connected to the Jewish community. Others advocate complimentary memberships in synagogues for intermarried couples, tickets to the High Holidays for intermar-ried children of congregation members, complimentary subscrip-tions to synagogue newsletters and other Jewish publications, and so on. Rabbis understand that participation costs may be the tip-ping factor against intermarried couples participating, especially those who are marginal in their commitment, feeling alienated from the Jewish community, looking for excuses not to belong or being ideologically opposed to the cost requirements to partici-pate in religious life. Some rabbis see synagogue costs as a real barrier, both for in-married and intermarried couples. Removing financial inhibitions can be effective in recruiting individuals for participation in Jewish life, particularly the synagogue. Other rabbis see the cost as more of a psychological barrier. Individuals who are ambivalent about how they feel about Jewish life in general and joining a synagogue in particular, may not join because the cost tips the decision against participation. Offering financial incentives or removing the disincentives is seen as key by many rabbis as an institutional imperative to reach intermarried couples.

One set of strategies calls for targeting youth. For example, some rabbis want to develop high school youth groups with specific programming and education about interfaith issues, marriage, Jewish identity and the phenomenon of being a Jew in a multicultural society. They believe that addressing the issue head-on in the language and context of the youths themselves is an important step in the education process. Others believe that these efforts also need to be expanded at the college level with rabbis speaking to college audiences in general where Jews are likely to attend on such subjects as contemporary Jewish values, on God or Judaism in contemporary American life, and so on.

The focus on youth also includes young singles. Some rabbis want to focus on helping singles find Jewish marriage partners. Monthly services, seders, special services clubs, recreational programs and so on, should be designed for Jewish singles where they may meet potential Jewish mates. This prevention strategy is less concerned with educational outcomes and more concerned with social realities. Jews are more likely to marry other Jews if they have the opportunity to meet them. Singles programs fall within prevention strategies, but represent a shift from a merely strengthening identity tactic to a strengthening opportunity tactic.

Some rabbis advocate building the Jewish community in general, thereby providing a positive context for individuals to be Jewish. Most rabbis understand the need for an overall communal strategy to building identity and encouraging involvement in Jewish life. This involves pro-active thinking and action on the part of federations, Jewish community centers, membership organizations and the vast range of organizations and institutions that serve the Jewish community. Because most rabbis believe that intermarriage is a structural outcome of the overall integration of Jews into American society, solutions are generally sought as a communal endeavor.

What Roles Do Rabbis Think They Should Play?

Any of the strategies that rabbis recommend require or suggest certain rabbinic roles. This is especially true in community building. In a recent survey in Northern California, rabbis were asked: "What role do you believe the rabbi should play in the community-planning process?" One of the roles identified for the rabbi was to serve as visionaries. They would help articulate the vision of the Jewish community, both within the congregation and to the Jewish community as a whole. The role of visionary requires the rabbi to consider what the Jewish community ought to be, both in terms of tradition and goals for the future.

The second role for rabbis is advocacy for the synagogue as an institution. As one Orthodox rabbi states, "the synagogue must re-emerge as the primary Jewish institution in the local community. This role must be both internal and external vis-à-vis the synagogue. The rabbi must ensure that the synagogue is worthy of its place in the community." As an advocate within the Jewish organizational and institutional structure, the rabbi must be able to articulate a vision for the synagogue and its role to integrate that vision into the community structure.

This calls the third role of the rabbi as political activist. Many believe the rabbi should encourage and recruit synagogue members for work in the community and themselves serve on local agency boards, including the Federation. Those who promote this role believe that rabbis should advise the Federation and other organizations about synagogue-related matters and matters of concern to the Jewish community in general. As advocates they would "play a strong and participating role in planning and advocating for outreach and marketing the synagogue as a resource for building knowledge and community," as one Reconstructionist contends. The role of political advocate makes rabbis ideological leaders who play prominent roles that are external to the synagogue and extend to the community planning process. As one Conservative rabbi stated: "Rabbis play a central planning role in their congregations. I believe that my goals are directed not only to my congregants but to the broader Jewish community as well. My vision must be incorporated into the broader planning process." This may lead to a coalition of rabbis, and as one rabbi advocates, we must "work in a non-denominational manner with lay leaders of Federation and auxiliary agencies." One Reform rabbi was advocating for rabbinic power and influence that demands some consensus and creating a collective voice. Another Reform rabbi indicated that rabbis should be on allocations committees, education committees and community relations councils. As active participants in Jewish life, they believe they have a great deal to add to the agenda of preservation and growth in the Jewish community.

The fourth role many rabbis cited was as the "wise person" that comes both from knowledge of traditional Judaism and working most intimately with large numbers of Jews. Rabbis see themselves as reservoirs of wisdom, as spiritual leaders of the community, knowledgeable about Jewish law and the interpretation of Jewish values to the Jewish community as a whole. By playing this role they create a stronger fabric in Jewish life and act as advocates for a stronger and more vibrant Jewish community.

Many rabbis believe their roles as community leaders are reinforced by a stronger institutional presence for the synagogue. The synagogue is seen as providing, as one Reform rabbi indicated, "a significant proportion of committed Jewish leadership." But other rabbis believe that particular synagogues need to focus internally, strengthening their own institutional planning. "We don't really have the energy to be involved in the bigger world." After getting his particular house in order, however, this rabbi wants to "figure a way to get my lay people more involved in the Jewish world outside the synagogue." This comes first from building a position of strength within the synagogue. Others believe that, as one Reform rabbi states, "Every *shul* should have a dialogue with community agencies on an ongoing basis through rabbinical leadership, lay and board leadership." He goes on to say that synagogues have been the institutional foundation of the Jewish community and this needs to be reasserted. Or as another rabbi puts it, the synagogue plays a central role in community affairs and planning, and the rabbi and the synagogue should "be involved with most areas of the Jewish community, especially if one assumes that synagogue members are involved in other areas of the Jewish community. I believe in the concept of *kehillah*," this rabbi states, "where there is a true 'federation' of Jewish communal institutions." Some rabbis are very specific about what the roles of the synagogue and the rabbi should be in community affairs and planning. One Reform rabbi states that it is the role of both to: 1) recruit and train community leaders; 2) provide space and volunteers for community events; 3) initiate joint synagogue and community programs. The need to build the capacity of the synagogue and then to build the capacity of the community is stated by more than one rabbi. As one indicates, "My synagogue is small and very insular. We need the expertise and aid of more centralized agencies. My synagogue would be consumers rather than creators. In contrast, we are good at small group involvement and helping people to feel safe about being Jewish. Some rabbis see congregational efforts as inseparable from other community endeavors because the implications of what goes on in the synagogue affects everyone, whether they are congregants or not, or whether or not a program or effort is specifically initiated by the synagogue. Another rabbi says, "In order to achieve the goal of a more cohesive Jewish community, rabbis believe that a number of important institutional/organizational changes would have to take place. Part of the communal agenda should be reaching out to the unaffiliated." One Reform rabbi believes that the community as a whole needs to "create a mechanism for servicing those who are unaffiliated with a synagogue in a way that shifts the sole burden of Jewish involvement from the synagogue, but hopefully moves people to eventual affiliation." In other words, there are multiple avenues for involvement, and the synagogue cannot and should not be solely responsible for bringing people into Jewish life. However, rabbis believe that ultimately everyone should belong to a synagogue or at least participate in synagogue life in some way.

The Rabbinic Call for Community Building

When asked what they believe to be the two or three most important needs for the local Jewish community, a few rabbis listed specific human service programs such as senior services, programs for AIDS patients and so on. But the vast majority listed the need for community-building programs that would help people develop a stronger Jewish identity. Almost all called for programs that would reach out to the unaffiliated and develop programming for marginal Jews. Specific kinds of programs and personnel to achieve this goal were also listed, including community chaplains, adequately paid teachers and expanded youth programming that is Israel-oriented. When asked what they believe to be the biggest problem facing American Jews today nearly all the rabbis who were surveyed said assimilation, lack of Jewish identity, poor Jewish education and insufficient knowledge of Judaism. Each of these was seen as a symptom of the other or a cause of the other, a general decline in the quality of the religious aspects of Jewish life. Most rabbis believe that even if most Jews were not Torah scholars, they could *daven* to some minimum degree, would fast on *Yom Kippur*, keep a kosher home, would say *kaddish* if a parent dies and otherwise maintain a level of Jewish identity and behavior that distinguished them as Jews in some fundamental way. The malaise that most rabbis identify as the major problem of contemporary Jewish life is in some sense independent of the intermarriage phenomenon. That is, intermarriage may result from this general low quality of Jewish life, but their feelings would be essentially the same even if Jews were marrying other Jews and exhibited the same low level of commitment to Jewish life and the same lack of understanding of what it means to be a Jew. Intermarriage is the most visible sign of what they believe to be the major problem facing American Jews, but it only reveals the decline of Jewish identity in other realms.

Most rabbis, therefore, in analyzing the character of the problem of intermarriage today ultimately believe it reflects the general assimilation of American Jews and the loss of Jewish identity as a whole. The distinction is critically important since most rabbis do not believe intermarriage to be the cause of the loss of Jewish identity, but rather a symptom. They tend to be optimistic in the ideological, institutional and programmatic approaches to dealing with intermarriage. For the most part, they truly believe that if they strengthen the core of Jewish life then the issue of intermarriage would become less problematic. On the one hand, more Jews would marry other Jews. On the other, a vibrant, attractive and meaningful Judaism would also appeal to the partners who do marry someone who is not Jewish.

CHAPTER 4

IMPLICATIONS FOR THE JEWISH COMMUNITY

THE NEED FOR A STRONG RABBINATE

D ebate among rabbis about intermarriage is a micro-cosm of the Jewish community's struggle with this issue. Jewish organizations and institutions view intermarriage as a threat to group survival. The rabbinic dialogue also reflects the conflict within individual families, where mothers, fathers, grandparents and the marriage partners themselves are uncertain about how to respond to the issue. Two different kinds of questions emerge from the analysis of rabbinic views toward intermarriage: What are the implications concerning rabbis as a group, and how should the community deal with the critical issue of intermarriage? Because the role of the rabbi is so central, the actions of the rabbinate require rethinking and reassessing. At the same time, other organizational and institutional approaches also need rethinking, separate from the specific role of the rabbi. The question of intermarriage goes to the heart of redefining the rabbinate and the Jewish community for the next century. This concluding chapter discusses the implications of the data, but not necessarily from the views of the rabbis themselves. Most importantly, it discusses the implications about what the community needs to think about in terms of the rabbis' role in approaching intermarriage, rather than an analysis of how to approach intermarriage in general.

It is important to reemphasize that rabbis are not responsible for "solving" the intermarriage "problem." Their role is central but not monolithic. They are very influential, but ought not be expected to act as magicians in dealing with the dilemmas associated with intermarriage. The potential for their influence, both positive and negative, however, can be enormous. They can help remake institutions and the policies that they implement. The rabbis themselves touch a myriad of Jewish issues. As a group they have more to say about the subject than any other professional and lay leaders in American Jewish life and their collective actions have more immediate and long-term effects. Even more importantly, if the role of the rabbi changes, the collective influence of the rabbinate can be even greater than it is today.

The suggestions for change outlined in Chapter 3 by the rabbis cover the usual answers given by rabbis, Jewish communal professionals and most lay leadership to deal with intermarriage. On the one hand, there is a call for programs that help involve Jews in existing institutions through a series of generally accepted programmatic interventions. Some rabbis speak primarily of building programs within, strengthening the core of Jewish life by concentrating on the most interested and committed Jews. Others advocate a variety of programs targeted for more "problematic" segments of Jewish society — the young, the unmarried, the intermarried. Some advocate religious teaching and others advocate social action or the provision of human services. Most rabbis envision remedies that operate within a narrow band of synagogue life as an institution as it is currently constructed. Furthermore, the roles that they see themselves playing are also closely tied to the current institutional structure.

There is a wide range of opinions, a great divergence among rabbis between denominations, within denominations, by age, experience and gender, by region and life experience on how they feel about intermarriage and how to deal with intermarriage. The diversity of opinion suggests multiple strategies and approaches to deal with the issue of intermarriage, and equally diverse roles for the rabbinate.

Their greatest rabbinic intervention may be on a one-to-one basis, cumulative with one Jewish individual after another over many years. Few Jews are untouched by their contact with a rabbi. Some are warm and loving, some are colder and more formal. Some are welcoming, some are forbidding. Some are extremely bright and visionary thinkers, and some are more mundane. But the rabbis are correct in their assessment that the future of Judaism in this country rests in the ability to formulate a vision, create an institutional structure and execute ideologies through programs that will help build Jewish community, identity and participation. The need for a forward-thinking, creative, charismatic rabbinate is an essential ingredient in building the Jewish community of the future. A creatively trained rabbinate is essential. Rabbis are correct in their assessment that the community must rethink how to provide more opportunities for positive interaction with Jewish life, and the means to develop a Judaism that is positive and relevant in an assimilated society.

This same logic holds true for the rabbis themselves. The community needs to rethink how rabbis are trained, what kinds of support they are given, how to attract and retain competent, charismatic thinkers and knowledgeable doers in both the congregational and the non-congregational setting. The data show a profession that is struggling. It follows that professional training and support is an issue that therefore must be addressed. Few rabbis discuss their own role as players, shapers and actors in the system, and how they are either facilitators or barriers to building stronger Jewish community. They recognize their potential positive role, but are more reluctant to discuss their potential negative role. The religious tradition in America favors the charismatic preacher and activist. American Jews may require no less. How the rabbinate attracts and holds the best and the brightest, the most interesting and the most creative, the most attractive and the most exciting is one of the challenges of contemporary Judaism. Certainly, Judaism can be relevant, purposeful and invigorating for many Jews who are unfamiliar with the benefits and fulfillment that come from a Jewish life. But who will teach them? If we accept the view that most parents and grandparents are unable, or unwilling, to provide this education, then the responsibility will fall more and more to institutions and the people who lead those institutions. Sociologists and rabbis alike can claim that Judaism will only be redeemed if parents and grandparents are committed to their children's Jewish education and upbringing, when in fact a high proportion of them may be unwilling or unable to do so. Jews do drop their children off for religious school, they do expect miraculous interventions and inspiration from the formal structure to maintain their children's Jewish life. But this miracle will not occur. A basic rebuilding of the Jewish community is necessary. What the rabbis intuitively and experientially recognize are fundamental weaknesses in the current structure of the American Jewish community.

The Need to Build the Rabbinate

Who will provide that guidance and lead the efforts to rebuild the community? The rabbinate is central to any efforts to rebuild the Jewish community. The general community has to provide the resources, both within the congregation and outside the congregation, to create a cadre of visionary, inspirational rabbis who will help mold the Jewish community of the future. Where such rabbis already exist, the Jewish community must provide the resources to free their time for the purpose of teaching, recruiting and organizing the Jewish community. Some of these tasks obviously can be performed by lay leadership, Jewish educators, social workers and others. But rabbis still command respect because they are rabbis and there is still an expectation that they will be teachers and "official" representatives of the Jewish tradition.

They can partner with key lay people, but these individuals have other professions. The Jewish community requires a host of individuals devoted to building Jewish life and learning. Therefore, the community needs to invest the resources in the training and support of individuals who will play this role in Jewish life.

No problem can be solved through a single set of actions or strategies. Issues concerning assimilation and intermarriage are systemically bound to a host of factors. It is not likely that much progress will be made in the preservation and renewal of Jewish life for large numbers of Jews unless there is a more actively supported, encouraged and enlivened rabbinate. As it currently stands, most rabbis lack a cohesive ideology, set of tools or set of practices to deal with the complex set of issues surrounding intermarriage. They are locked, as the community as a whole is locked, in old debates. The data show that they are grappling. Ambivalence is more prevalent than any other feeling and approaches to the issue tend to be narrowly circumscribed. Most are constrained by their denominational ideologies for formulating their own sets of activities and actions within their denominations or individual congregations. Many need to be trained to be more sensitive in dealing with prospective intermarried couples. Many of their writings come through as somewhat harsh. They need to have a network of support for discussion and policy formulation, both within the congregation and outside the congregation, for the myriad of issues surrounding inreach and outreach to intermarried couples and their families. Some are doing quite well, others may be adding to the problem. Rabbis feel besieged and responsible because they are both. The rabbinate and rabbis need help if both are going to help build the Jewish community of the future.

This, of course, will require remaking the rabbinate. Some proportion of rabbis can fulfill their communal role and some cannot. The community cannot afford any mediocre rabbinic leadership. A great weeding out must take place over the next

decade with an eye toward reshaping the makeup of the rabbinate. The community should also recruit and support non-congregational rabbis to serve the community as teachers and orga-
nizers. These rabbis can be supported by philanthropists, foundations and federations. They should be located throughout the
United States to serve Jews who do not choose to be part of congregations. *Havurot,* study groups and other modes of religious
interaction must be acceptable as well. The community needs to
recruit and support rabbis to serve those who choose alternate
methods of religious identity and participation. At the same time,
synagogue-based rabbis also need support, especially in dealing
with intermarriage. They need new skills and new ideology. They
cannot be on the defensive most of the time, because it makes
their approach to Judaism defensive.

One of the key functions of rabbis will be to provide inspiration, guidance and training for those who wish to convert to
Judaism. Those who convert often respond to the mentoring and
leadership of some particular rabbi. The community's greatest
institutional approach to intermarriage could be the availability
of hundreds of rabbis, who, through their institutional and individual efforts, attract hundreds of thousands of non-Jews to
choose Judaism as their way of life and teach them to participate.
The battle of intermarriage will be won in an open and pluralistic society, not through retreat and rejection, but through internal
communal strength that encourages and welcomes others to be
Jews. This ideology does not call for abandonment of standards.
Indeed, it requires the opposite. But the administration of standards must be done with care and concern and invitation and
challenge to participate because Judaism is a rich and rewarding
experience.

Rebuilding the community offers an attractive alternative in
an American society that longs for and seeks to establish a
stronger sense of belonging. Judaism can offer this, but only
through rebuilding from within with a clear sense of purpose and

standards. But no one should have to prove that they wish to participate in Judaism; no one's sincerity should be questioned. An inquiry or an expression of interest should be met with enthusiasm and passion. Rabbis must be prepared to take every inquiry about Judaism seriously and proceed to inculcate and incorporate on the assumption that the interest is real until proven otherwise. The interviews show that this is the opposite approach of many rabbis, who make conversion difficult. This is ultimately destructive to the growth of the Jewish community.

Other Jewish communal leaders and professionals provide some of the support for rebuilding the Jewish community. But an informed, educated, enthusiastic rabbinate is an important key to rebuilding the Jewish community and addressing the issue of group survival and the possible threat intermarriage poses to that survival. This book looks at how rabbis feel about intermarriage because, in the end, they are the most important players in this drama. Sadly, many are emotionally ill-equipped or intellectually unprepared to deal with this complex problem. They are too confused or angry themselves to help others. Largely, the Jewish public and the organizational and institutional structure, including the synagogue, have placed them as either gate-keepers or lightning rods, leaving them to their own internal struggles to face an impossible situation. The community and the rabbis themselves are forced to deal with the intermarriage issue as if it were isolated from the greater set of issues surrounding community building and involvement. We need a different approach, a different ideology, and in some cases a different set of individuals to deal with this issue or at least a different set of retraining mechanisms and supports to deal with the issue. No program or set of programs, no level of Jewish education or type of Jewish education can either prevent intermarriage or make people Jewish through osmosis. A reinvigorated and inspired rabbinate is the best hope for the future of the Jewish community.

Retraining the Rabbinate

The professional training, development and support of rabbis are key areas of concern that emerge from the discussions. For example, are rabbis sufficiently trained to deal with issues surrounding intermarriage? They must face complex interactions with congregants, individuals seeking advice and counseling, confused parents or uncertain marriage partners at times of emotional crisis. Individuals interact with rabbis in a highly charged environment surrounding wedding ceremonies, baby namings, *bar* and *bat mitzvahs*, and deaths. Indeed, by definition, the circumstances are almost always complex and emotionally charged since they either involve special life-cycle events, familial or religious concerns, or both. Issues surrounding intermarriage are almost always stressful or crisis-oriented because individuals are often seeking guidance or resolution about something that is either of primal importance to them or a family member. Individual Jews often experience the same level of emotional confusion, conflict and intensity that rabbis themselves experience about this issue. Yet perceptions of individuals about the correct course of action are often at odds with the rabbi. How equipped are rabbis to deal with these emotions, traumas and the anguish? These issues are qualitatively different than illness or death or other emotionally charged problems. Respective denominational movements, seminaries and peer groups must prepare rabbis and support them to address these issues.

Dealing with intermarriage requires a sophisticated set of mediation, counseling and leadership skills. The seminaries that train rabbis should have specific and expansive teaching tracks on dealing with intermarriage. This is true for the Orthodox and Conservative institutions as well as the Reform. Just because the Orthodox and Conservative communities do not formally permit rabbis to perform intermarriages is irrelevant to the need for careful training and guidance for rabbis. How does one respond to a request to perform an intermarriage ceremony in a way that encourages the couple to participate in Judaism as opposed to driving them away? How does the rabbi encourage participation in the synagogue? How does the rabbi move individuals toward a Jewish identity and conversion to Judaism? For the most part, the communal debate focuses, and the internal debate of the rabbi as well, on what the answers should be to specific requests for rabbinic involvement in interfaith wedding ceremonies or official policies of synagogues. Because the emotional issues are so complex, however, the focus needs to shift from answers to the questions themselves and how rabbis deal with those questions. Perhaps there should be less concern in teaching rabbis whether to say yes or not to performing an intermarriage or allowing non-Jewish congregants to be members of synagogues, and so on, and more concern as to *how* they say it and how they interact with individuals and families. Styles of interaction, modes of inquiry, revealed levels of compassion and understanding are all as important as, and perhaps more important than the action of the rabbi in any specific instance. Because rabbis play the role of therapist, physician and policeman as well as that of spiritual leader, they must be trained for the roles into which they are thrust daily. Seminary and *yeshiva* curricula should include role-playing with couples seeking an intermarriage ceremony, training in counseling and thorough ideological underpinnings with which the rabbi can be comfortable, and which support him or her in interacting with the Jewish public.

Rabbis in the Reform movement need the most support. In some sense, the movement has left them in the most vulnerable positions, allowing individual discretion on whether or not to perform wedding ceremonies for intermarried couples, the most contentious issue between congregants and rabbis. The Conservative and Orthodox rabbis are powerless within their denominational structure to make choices. In some sense the analysis suggests that many rabbis are ill-prepared by the institutions that train them to cope with the complex environment in which they must operate. They are involved in a communal mael- strom that requires special interpersonal skills. Training concern- ing intermarriage raises another whole set of questions about rabbinic training in general for congregational leadership, com- munity roles and responsibilities.

Rabbis require opportunities for collegial support and peer group interaction. They are faced with constant moral dilemmas, personal responsibilities and attacks and a sense of isolation. Peer group counseling, workshops and seminars, and other such types of support need to be readily available to rabbis on the front lines. Such opportunities need to be available at the local, regional and national levels. While everyone can come to talk to the rabbi, to whom can the rabbi talk? Such support and counseling may be necessary for a wide variety of issues in the rabbis' lives beyond intermarriage, and perhaps it may be even more necessary for other issues. But there are few areas that put the rabbi in as much conflict with other rabbis and with congregants. The intermar- riage issue may demonstrate a lack of collegial support in general and institutional support in particular for rabbis dealing with complex problems. This is not to say, of course, that local boards of rabbis do not exist and meet and offer some venue for discus- sion and interchange. However, these tend to be substantive and political, not personal. The need for personal support is essential. Dealing with individuals about intermarriage issues is often a therapeutic process. Rabbis need their own batteries recharged and their own therapeutic venue to be more effective. In short, rabbis appear ill-prepared before they get into the field, and gen- erally isolated while approaching difficult everyday decisions. It is possible, of course, for rabbis to form their own support groups, but this may be viewed as a sign of either professional or ideolog- ical weakness. It is really a denominational and communal responsibility, both in the training and ongoing support since the issue is communal as well as personal. The retreats that were held to discuss the issue of intermarriage in Northern California, for example, were heavily attended and were highly emotional events. The retreats revealed deep needs for opportunities for time to pause, reflect and discuss this important issue. Such venues should be available on an ongoing basis, funded by congregations, federations and foundations. Rabbis rarely have the opportunity to retreat from the pressures and stresses of everyday life to interact with each other, learn from one another, and help each other to face complex issues concerning intermarriage or other community problems. These seminars, retreats and workshops should be fully funded in terms of accommodation, supporting resources, personnel and all aspects of these activities. The need for these opportunities goes far beyond the traditional views of professional development or human resource investment. The community needs to help the rabbis help the community.

Rabbis as Communal Leaders

What should be the rabbinic role in the intermarriage debate? First and foremost, the role of the rabbi should be to provide leadership. Leadership takes a variety of forms. Collectively, the rabbinate has to provide standards concerning intermarriage. They ultimately have to say which actions are right or wrong, and just as importantly, they have to be able to say why. That not all rabbis agree and that there are denominational differences is an accepted tenet of American Judaism and fits well within the pluralistic character and ideology of American Jews. A variety of options and interpretations is expected since American Judaism is not monolithic and the rabbinate is not a hierarchical authority. A single edict about intermarriage would not fit into the realities of contemporary American Jewish life. On the other hand, rabbis cannot be effective leaders if they are acting only on personal philosophy and belief. Their beliefs and actions must be tied to a greater set of laws and guidelines that have both theological and communal roots and support. The leadership that comes from setting standards must be accompanied by leadership in explaining those standards. American Jews are highly educated. They need to understand the historical and religious antecedents to any particular approach to dealing with intermarriage. Rabbis can exert leadership by explaining their ideology and its roots in either traditional or evolving Judaism. Indeed, rabbis will earn more respect and exert more influence by being well grounded and having the ability to explain and translate that grounding to the Jewish public. The presentation of standards must be accomplished, however, through teaching and counseling, and not through rejection. Standards and rejection often go hand in hand in the minds of the Jewish public, more as a matter of style and approach of many rabbis rather than substance. Rabbis must be careful in how they apply standards and the messages they transmit about their views. Leadership comes primarily through education, compassion and integrity, not threats or unusual use of power.

Leadership also comes through vision. The adherence to standards must not only have historical and theological antecedents, it must also be connected to some greater vision of the future of the Jewish community. Standards must be connected to other sets of actions that move the community forward. The rabbis must not only say what they will not do, but what they will do to help individuals who are struggling with conflicts associated with intermarriage. If rabbis are prepared to say, for example, that they will not marry an intermarried couple they must also say that they are willing to educate, counsel and otherwise help to involve the couple as they struggle with issues of dual identity. All actions must be tied to some cohesive vision of what the rabbi and the community are attempting to accomplish. Inmarriage for its own sake cannot be a driving or compelling ideology. The standards have to signify some desire for a cohesive and vibrant Jewish community. This is difficult to communicate in times of emotional trauma, but nevertheless essential. Articulating a vision of the Jewish community has to go hand-in-hand with all rabbinic actions concerning intermarriage. And the vision must be positive. Individuals cannot respond to implications or threats that they are being bad Jews, bad individuals or that somehow they are personally responsible for the destruction of Jewish life. Rabbis must be able to communicate their own personal responsibility and each individual's responsibility as a member of the Jewish community. Some individuals, of course, will condemn rabbis no matter what they do when they disagree with a rabbi's decision that affects them personally. Some will react negatively to the establishment of any standards, or when those standards are applied to them as individuals. But most individuals can respond with respect and understanding if they feel they have been treated that way. Most individuals will respond positively to a rabbi's leadership putting forth a positive vision of what the Jewish community ought to be, but the vision must involve passion and compassion as well as grounding. Most of the teaching, therefore, must come at times other than crisis moments in individuals' lives. Rabbis have to have increasing opportunities to teach their philosophy of Jewish life to as many individuals as possible. This must take place both within and outside of the congregational setting. Rabbis need to be community teachers, exerting their leadership through positing and inspiring an attractive vision of Jewish life. The issue of intermarriage is inextricably bound with the overall constructs of the Jewish community, its attractiveness and cohesiveness in the minds of Jews.

Rabbis must also exert their influence as community activists both within the synagogue and outside the synagogue. If the community is to devise an agenda for building identity and participation, rabbis must be key designers and implementers in the system. They need to build coalitions and direct resources from a common set of goals and visions about what the Jewish community ought to be. They must be proactive in guiding people to what they should do. Arguing against intermarriage does not provide much leadership or vision. It only puts a negative spin on what it means to be a Jew and induces guilt and anxiety among those who are seeking marriage partners or who have already chosen one who was not born Jewish. Rabbis cannot be keepers of the faith through a message of exclusion, even if they wish to promote exclusivity. These are two very different concepts: One suggests membership for an elite and the other barriers to the unacceptable. Pluralism in the United States thrives upon an illusion of universal equality while promoting exclusive participation in desirable neighborhoods, clubs, economic groups or professions. All aspects of American society are theoretically open to all who earn some right to participate or exhibit some level of commitment or willingness to share, sacrifice or otherwise pay for their membership. Judaism can and should exact some price for participating as an incentive or prize, but it cannot *a priori* tell everyone that they are automatically excluded as a matter of birthright. Like most other religions, Judaism does have a path to conversion, a set of standards to be followed for one to participate and be accepted as part of the group. Rabbis can argue that Jews should marry other Jews, whether by birth or conversion. Anyone can be a Jew. The process of making Jews is a key area of rabbinic influence and one where they can be much more proactive.

The intermarriage "crisis" can pervade the American Jewish psyche. But should it? There is an alternative to panic. We need to develop creative ways of rethinking the meaning and purpose of Jewish conversion. Rabbis must be an integral part of this evolution. Some rabbis will lead the change effort, others will have to be led. Rabbis, as part of a complex social and religious system, are diversified by ideology, training, the communal hats they wear and the roles they play in Jewish life. Creative approaches will involve rabbis in different ways — some will conceptualize what to do and some will invent the institutions to carry out new mandates.

Rabbis need emotional and institutional assistance and support to help create the next era in Jewish life. The burden of solving the "intermarriage crisis" cannot be laid at their feet. To be sure, what rabbis do is critical. But so is what parents, philanthropists, synagogues, seminaries and federations choose to do.

Rabbis struggle daily with questions of Jewish survival and growth. This book shows the range of strong feelings they have about the quality and future of Jewish life. They reflect the heart and soul of Jews everywhere; in the end, they are most extraordinary in how ordinary they are.

The rabbis' words in this book are a reflection of the landscape of thoughts and feelings of American Jews in general. Contradictions, confusion, confounding dilemmas emerge — no simple questions, no simple answers, no one to blame. Therefore, this book calls for compassion — in understanding rabbis' feelings as they confront assimilation, in sorting through our personal views about Jews and non-Jews marrying one another, and compassion in considering alternative ways of renewing modern Judaism.

GLOSSARY

Aliyah (pl., *aliyot*) "Going up, ascending." (1) The honor of being called up to recite a blessing before the reading of the Torah portion, and 2) immigration to Israel

Asher bachar banu "Who has chosen us"

Asher kidshanu b'mitzvotav "Who sanctified us by the commandments"

Aufrufin Traditionally, the bridegroom's *aliyah* to the Torah on the Sabbath prior to his wedding. In non-orthodox synagogues today, the bride often has an *aliyah* as well

Bar mitzvah (pl., *b'nai mitzvah*) "Son of the commandment." The age at which a Jewish boy becomes responsible for his actions. Also the ceremony celebrating this occasion by reading from the Torah and *Haftarah* usually during the Saturday morning service. This is generally held around his thirteenth birthday

Bat mitzvah (pl., *b'not mitzvah*) "Daughter of the commandment." The age at which a Jewish girl becomes responsible for her actions. Also the ceremony celebrating this occasion by reading from the Torah and *Haftarah* usually during the Saturday morning service. This is generally held around her twelfth or thirteenth birthday

B'diavad "After the fact"

Beit din Three-person rabbinic court, guided by the principles of *halacha*. May be convened for the purpose of overseeing a conversion ceremony, to prepare a Jewish writ of divorce or to serve as a mediating body in a dispute between two Jews

Beshert Destined by divine providence

Bimah (1) The dais in a sanctuary from which the Torah is read and where the leader of the service stands when leading services; (2) the front platform of a synagogue where the ark containing the Torah stands

Brit milah (*bris* — traditional) The covenant of circumcision — ritual circumcision of male children at eight days old, symbolizing the covenant between God and Abraham

Chanukah (*hanukkah*) The eight day Festival of Lights, commemorating the Maccabean victory over the Greco-Syrian religious oppression, and the subsequent rededication of the temple in Jerusalem. Usually falls in December

Chupah (*huppah*) Jewish marriage canopy

Daven To pray

Erev "Evening." All Jewish holidays begin at sundown the evening before a holiday

Etrog A citron, one of the four species used ritually on Sukkot

Gemara Major rabbinic commentary on the Mishna, the major part of the Talmud

Ger (pl., *gerim*) Convert

Gerut Conversion

Ger toshav "Fellow traveler." Partial proselyte or someone who has not formally converted to Judaism

Halftarah "Conclusion." The prophetic section recited after the reading of the Torah on Sabbaths, festivals and other occasions

Halacha The Talmudic code; a generic term for the whole legal system of Judaism, encompassing all the laws and observances

Hashem A name for God, used by those who do not want to take God's Hebrew name "in vain"

Havurah (pl., *havurot*) A group or fellowship specifically organized around prayer, study, celebration of Jewish holidays, spiritual and/or social purposes

Hillel Jewish organizations that serve college and university students on campuses

Kaddish (*Mourner's Kaddish*) Traditional prayer affirming life, recited by mourners

Kashrut The Jewish dietary laws

Kehillah Community

Ketubah The Jewish marriage contract

Kiddush The blessing over wine for meals, *Shabbat*, festivals and holy days

Kosher Prepared in accordance with Jewish law, most often referring to food

L'chat'chila "Before the fact"

L'ma'an hayeladim "For the sake of the children"

Lehrhaus (*Judaica*) An organization offering adult Jewish education classes in the San Francisco Bay Area

Lulav A palm branch used on Sukkot

Midrash (*midrashic*) Rabbinic commentaries to the bible

Mikvah A ritual bath used for purification purposes by married women after menstruation, by brides before nuptials and by converts at the culmination of the conversion ceremony

Minyan Quorum of ten Jewish adults necessary for a public prayer service. The *minyan* represents the Jewish people as a community

Mishagas Craziness

Mitzvah (pl., *mitzvot*) A commandment, positive or negative; one of the 613 Torah-given precepts or one of the rabbinic commandments added later; also loosely refers to a "good deed"

Oneg Shabbat "Sabbath joy." A celebration following Friday evening services which may include refreshments, singing and dancing

Pesach (Passover) The holiday celebrating the Exodus of the Israelites from Egypt

Rabbonim Rabbinical community

Rosh Hashanah The Jewish New Year

Seder Ritual meal at Passover

Shabbat (*Shabbos* — traditional) The Sabbath, the day of rest; the seventh day of the week. Begins at sundown Friday and ends at sundown on Saturday

Simcha A joyous occasion

Shavuot (Pentecost, the Festival of Weeks) Celebrates the giving of the Torah at Mount Sinai

Shivah The first seven days of mourning

Sukkot (*Feast of the Tabernacles*) One of the three ancient harvest and pilgrimage festivals (with *Pesach* and *Shavuot*); the thanksgiving and harvest holiday that occurs five days after *Yom Kippur*

Synagogue (*shul* — Yiddish) House of worship

Tallit A ritual prayer shawl

Talmud (*Talmudic*) A compilation of Rabbinic teachings, comprising the *Mishna* and the *Gemara*, which expands the *Mishna*

Torah (1) The five books of Moses; (2) the sacred texts of Judaism

Yeshiva An academy for the study of Torah

Yom Kippur (*Day of Atonement*) The holiest day of the Jewish religious year, the last day of the Ten Days of Penitence. A fast day, during which the Jew seeks forgivenessness for sins

REFERENCES

Rabbis' Sermons

Abrahamson, Elka, and Judy Shanks. "This Changing Autumn Clubhouse." Peninsula Temple Beth El, San Mateo, California, September 1991.

Adland, Jonathan F. "The Challenges to Reform Judaism." Temple Adath Israel, Lexington, Kentucky, September 1993.

___. "Intermarriage." Temple Adath Israel, Lexington, Kentucky, September 1991.

Asher, Raphael. "Erev Rosh Hashanah." Congregation B'nai Tikvah, Walnut Creek, California, September 1986.

___. "Select Interfaith Weddings." Officiating at the Founding of a Jewish Home, undated.

Barenbaum, Michael. Untitled. Congregation Rodef Sholom, San Rafael, California, undated.

Baumgard, Herbert M. "Can a Rabbi Perform an Intermarriage?" Temple Beth Am, South Miami, Florida, January 1983.

Berman, Howard. "Open Hearts and an Open Door: A Reaffirmation of Ten Years of the Sinai Outreach Program." Chicago Sinai Congregation, 1991.

____. "Open Hearts and an Open Door: A Different Jewish Response to Intermarriage." Chicago Sinai Congregation, 1983.

Birnholz, Richard J. "Children of Intermarriages." Congregation Schaarai Zedek, Tampa, Florida, undated.

Brenner, Reeve Robert. "Jewish, Christian, or Chewish?" Bethesda Jewish Congregation, Bethesda, Maryland, September 1994.

Bronstein, Herbert. "Jews By Choice." North Shore Congregation Israel, Glencoe, Illinois, undated.

Cohen, Henry. "Why Not Judaism? The Challenge of Continuity and The Jewish Gestalt." Beth David Reform Congregation, Gladwyne, Pennsylvania, undated.

Friedman, Ronne. "To Rekindle the Flame." Temple Israel, Boston, Massachusetts, May 1994.

Garfein, Stanley J. "Never Just a Symbol." Temple Israel, Tallahassee, Florida, September 1993.

Ginsburg, Jonathan. "Conditions for the Jewish Survival." Temple of Aaron, St. Paul, Minnesota, Rosh Hashanah, 1991.

Glazier, James S. "Embracing the Jew and the Non-Jew." Temple Sinai, South Burlington, Vermont, October 1991.

Gluck, Arnold S. "Jewish Love Will Heal the Jewish People." Temple Beth-El, Somerville, New Jersey, 1994.

Herzbrun, Michael. "Yom Kippur." Temple Emanu-El of Irondequoit, Rhochester, New York, 1992.

Kadden, Bruce. "Intermarriage: Threat or Opportunity." Temple Beth El, Salinas, California, 1992.

Kahn, Bruce. "Intermarriage." Temple Shalom, Washington, D.C., December 1981.

Kingsley, Ralph P. "The Ties That Bind." September 1991.

Kline, David L. "Intermarriage." B'Nai Israel, Monroe, Louisiana, December 1990.

Kunis, Mark H. "Behar." Congregation Shearith Israel, Atlanta, Georgia, May 1993.

Lipof, Emily A. "The Challenge of Intermarriage." Temple B'nai Chaim, Georgetown, Connecticut, September 1991.

Lippman, Charles. "The Challenge of Intermarriage – Rosh Hashanah." Temple B'nai Chaim, Georgetown, Connecticut 1991.

Mahler, Mark J. "Intermarriage: Complex Questions, Clear Conclusions." Temple Emanuel, Pittsburgh, Pennsylvania, undated.

Mahrer, Larry. "Implications of the Jewish Population Study." Beth Israel Congregation, Florence, South Carolina, 1992.

Moline, Jack. "Ten Things Jewish Parents Don't Say Enough to Their Children." Agudas Achim Congregation, Alexandria, Virginia, 1991.

___. "Yom Kippur." Agudas Achim Congregation, Alexandria, Virginia, 1988.

Pernick, Daniel. "Yom Kippur 5752." Beth Am Temple, Pearl River, New York, 1991.

Rank, Perry R. "We Are All Jewish by Choice." Temple Beth Am, Springfield, New Jersey, October 1992.

Reiner, Fred W. "Yom Kippur Morning Sermon." Temple Sinai, Washington, D.C., September 1988.

___. "Yom Kippur Morning Sermon." Temple Sinai, Washington, D.C., September 1991.

Rosenberg, James B. "Interfaith Marriage: Challenge and Opportunity." Temple Habonim, Barrington, Rhode Island, September 1992.

Ross, Dennis. "When a Jew Intermarries." Temple Anshe Amunim, Pittsfield, Massachusetts, May 1994.

Rossoff, Donald B. "Intermarriage: Realities and Possibilities." Temple B'nai Or, Morristown, New Jersey, 1992.

Sonsino, Rifat. "Reflections on Interfaith Marriages." Temple Beth Shalom, Needham Heights, Massachusetts, 1991.

Stahl, Samuel M. "Three Ways to Practice Judaism: Belonging." Temple Beth-El, San Antonio, Texas, September 1991.

Arthur F. "Officiating at an Intermarriage: Another Rabbi's View." Temple Adath Yeshurun, Manchester, New York, undated.

Warmflash, Andrew C. "Kol Nidre 5749." Congregation B'nai Tikvah, North Brunswick, New Jersey, September 1988.

Zedek, Michael. "Yom Kippur Sermon – 5753." The Temple Congregation B'nai Jehudah, Kansas City, Missouri, October 1992.

Zelermyer, Gerald B. to Andrew Feinstein. "Letter Regarding Paper on Intermarriage." Emanuel Synagogue, West Hartford, Connecticut, May 1994.

Zimmerman, Marcia. "Opening the Doors." Temple Israel, Minneapolis, Minnesota, 1993.

ARTICLES AND PAPERS

bat Sarah, Khulda, and Moshe ben Asher. "Gather the People: Continuity Through Congregational Organizing." Novato, California (1995).

ben Asher, Moshe, and Khulda bat Sarah. "Jewish Out-Migration; Why is it happening and what should we do about it?" Novato, California (1994).

Berk, William C. *Chai Lights.* Temple Chai, Phoenix, Arizona (February 1991)

Brownstein, Marc. "What to Do About Interfaith Marriage." *Jewish Herald Voice*, Houston, Texas (1992).

Cohen, Henry. "Mixed Marriage and Jewish Continuity." *CCAR Journal* (April 1972): 48-54.

___. "Panel on Intermarriage." *Raayonot: A Newsletter of the Reconstructionist Rabbinical Association*, Vol. 1, No. 1 (1980): 8-15.

___. "Promises, Promises." *Moment* (February 1997): 56-57.

Cohen, Simcha J. "Reaction to Intermarriage Statistics — May a Jew Who Marries 'Out' Be Counted in a Minyan?" The R.C.A. Roundtable, Rabbinical Council of America, New York (1991).

Cohen, Steven M. "Why Intermarriage May Not Threaten Jewish Continuity." *Moment* (December 1994): 54-57.

Danziger, Harry K. "Why I Officiate at Selected Interfaith Weddings." *Reform Judaism* (Fall 1996): 52-54.

Fishbein, Irwin H. *Rabbinic Participation in Intermarriage Ceremonies.* Summary of Rabbinic Center for Research and Counseling 1995 Survey (29 December 1995).

___. *Intermarriage and Outreach: Facing Contemporary Challenges.* 24th Annual Convention of the Federation of Reconstructionist Congregations and Havurot (14 June 1984).

Geller, Stuart. "A Question About Wedding Blessings." *Temple Emanu-El Bulletin,* Vol. 60, No. 10:3 (1992).

Gerard, Jonathan H. "From the Rabbi's Study." Bulletin of Temple Berith Sholom, Troy, New York (1980).

Goldstein, Sidney, et al. "Twelve Angry Men And Women." *Moment* (April 1995): 66-67.

Gorin, Howard. "From the Rabbi." Series of articles, Beth Tikva, Rockville, Maryland (1992).

Greenstein, Howard. Unpublished letter, Congregation Ahavat Chesed, Jacksonville, Florida (1994).

Jacobs, Steven L. "Rabbinic Officiating at Mixed and/or Inter-Marriage." Position Paper, Congregation Sha'arei Shomayim, Mobile, Alabama, (October 1981).

Layman, Robert. "Conference on Intermarriage." Unpublished transcript, Conservative Movement of Greater Philadelphia, Philadelphia, Pennsylvania (November 1992).
Lerner, Stephen C. "Choosing Judaism, Issues Relating to Conversion." *Celebration and Renewal* (1993): 71-89.

Roberts, Daniel A. "Jewish Conscience Says 'No' to Performing Intermarriage." *Cleveland Jewish News* (12 February 1993): 12.

Schaktman, Peter B. "Rabbinic Officiation at Mixed Marriages." Unpublished paper, Congregation Emanu El, Houston, Texas (undated).

Schindler, Alexander M. Union of American Hebrew Congregations. *Outreach: The Case for a Missionary Judaism.* Presidential Address to the Board of Trustees, Houston, Texas (December 1978).

Schulweis, Harold. "Stranger in Our Mirror." *Inside Reform Judaism* (Fall 1989): 18-20.

___. "The Hyphen Between the Cross and the Star: Why Judaism and Christianity Don't Mix." *Reconstructionist* (undated): 8-12.

Segal, Jack. "How the Rabbi Kept His Vow Not to Sermonize on Interdating." *Page National* (June 1993): 8-14.

___. "The Rabbi's Message to His College Students." *Page National* (June, 1993): 8-9, 14.

Tendler, Moshe David. "An Alternate Analysis of the 'Intermarriage Statistics'; Not to Rebuke Is to Condone." Unpublished letter (April 1992).

Whitman, Michael. "Notes on Intermarriage." Unpublished letter, Young Israel of New Haven, New Haven, Connecticut (May 1994).

AUTHORS

Gary A. Tobin, Ph.D., is president of the Institute for Jewish & Community Research in San Francisco. He is also Director of the Leonard and Madlyn Abramson Program in Jewish Policy Research, Center for Policy Options at the University of Judaism in Los Angeles. He earned his Ph.D. in City and Regional Planning from the University of California at Berkeley. He was the Director for eleven years of the Maurice and Marilyn Cohen Center for Modern Jewish Studies at Brandeis University in Waltham, Massachusetts. Prior to joining Brandeis, Dr. Tobin spent eleven years at Washington University in St. Louis, and was the Director of the University College Urban Affairs Program.

Dr. Tobin has worked extensively in the area of patterns of racial segregation in schools and housing. He is the editor of two volumes about the effects of the racial schism in America, *What Happened to the Urban Crisis?* and *Divided Neighborhoods.*

Gary Tobin is the author of numerous books, articles, and planning reports on a broad range of subjects. He has published widely in the areas of Jewish organizational planning and philanthropy in the Jewish community. His books include *Jewish Perceptions of Antisemitism,* and *Opening the Gates: How Proactive Conversion Can Revitalize the Jewish Community.* Dr. Tobin is now working on a new book, *Philanthropy in the Modern Jewish Community.* He is currently involved in research concerning synagogue affiliation, racial and ethnic diversity in the Jewish community, and Jewish family foundations.

Gary and his wife Diane reside in San Francisco. They have six children, Adam, 29; Amy, 25; Sarah, 23; Aryeh, 21; Mia, 17 and Jonah, 2.

Katherine G. Simon, Ph.D., is currently the Director of Research and Professional Development for the Coalition of Essential Schools in Oakland, California. She is involved in research and professional development efforts for the national school reform movement. She received her Ph.D. in Education from Stanford University School of Education. She is the author of *The Place of Meaning: The Moral and Intellectual Life of High Schools*, New Haven: Yale University Press, 1999.

INDEX

A

Abba, Rabbi 128
Aliyah (pl., Aliyot) 129, 140
Asher bachar banu 133
Asher kidshanu b'mitzvotav 133
Asher, Rabbi Raphael 23-24, 95
Aufrufin 122

B

B'diavad 84-85
Bar mitzvah 11,60-61, 119, 132-134, 156
Bat mitzvah 11, 119, 132-134, 156
Beit din 104, 110
Berman, Rabbi Howard 24-25, 36-37, 39, 97-98, 137
Beshert 23
Bimah 132
Birnholz, Rabbi Richard 46-47
Bris (brit milah) 29, 99, 119
Brownstein, Rabbi Marc 36, 39, 42, 97

C

Cantor 37-38
Catholic 28, 30, 47
Ceremony 11, 13-14, 32, 37, 43, 78, 86, 89, 92-93, 99, 101, 108, 121, 157
Chanukah xiii
Circumcision 13, 104-105, 111

P
Pernick, Rabbi Daniel 54
Pesach (Passover) xiii, 140
Philanthropy 10, 154, 163
Prevention 6, 8-10, 32-33, 66, 139-142
Proselytizing 8- 9

R
Rabbonim 80
Reconstructionist xiv, 5, 12-13, 19, 139, 144
Reform xiv-xv, 5-6, 12, 14, 18-21, 25, 27-28, 30, 32-33, 36, 38-39,
    41, 43, 47, 49, 55-58, 62-65, 68, 71-74, 78, 87, 89-91, 93-
    95, 98-101, 103, 106-108, 114, 116, 119, 122-123, 130,
    133-136, 139, 144-146, 156-157
Reiner, Rabbi Fred 131
Ritual xv, 7, 30, 34, 44, 46, 82, 85, 96, 104, 129, 132-133, 140
Roberts, Rabbi Daniel 70-71
Rosenberg, Rabbi James 20, 70-71
Rosh Hashanah 19, 20, 22, 24, 70, 118, 137
Ross, Rabbi Dennis 50
Rossoff, Rabbi Donald 54, 69

S
Schindler, Rabbi Alexander 135
Seder 142
Segal, Rabbi Jack 55- 56, 115-116
Seminaries 10, 14, 35, 156-159, 163
Shabbat 53, 85, 89, 93, 104-105, 110, 135, 140
Shivah 36
Silver, Rabbi Samuel 37-38, 100
Simon, Rabbi Eliezer ben 128
Sonsino, Rabbi Rifat 51
Spiritual (sprituality) 8, 22, 106, 114, 144, 157
Stahl, Rabbi Samuel 59